Fur Kids

Fur Kids

A Life with Dogs

William L. Buchanan

Baylaurel Press
Mill Valley, California

Cover and interior design by Rob Roehrick

Editing by Lisa A. Smith

Photography by William L. Buchanan

Copyright 2007 by William L. Buchanan

ISBN 978-1-931093-02-6

Library of Congress Control Number: 2006909972

∞ The paper used in this publication meets the minimum
requirements of the American National Standard for
Information Sciences — Permanence of Paper for Printed
Library Materials, ANSI Z39.48-1992.

Baylaurel Press
775 E. Blithedale Ave. #251
Mill Valley, CA 94941

For Claire, my wife for thirty-seven years,
and the best friend that man or dog ever had

The author will contribute
a portion of the profits from the sale of this book
to canine rescue organizations.

Contents

Preface

9

Red

15

Maximillian of Marin

61

Blazer

95

Joey

155

Brady

191

About the Author

221

Preface

This book began its life in the year 2000 as *Living with Brittanys: A Survival Guide.* It was a chronicle of the three dogs of this unique breed that my wife, Claire, and I had owned until that time. After we adopted Joey and Brady from American Brittany Rescue, it became apparent that the old manuscript needed an extreme makeover: thus the book you're holding in your hands. But I should begin at the beginning.

Our first experience with Brittanys began not long after Claire and I met in 1968 at Stanford Research Institute in Menlo Park, California, where she was working as a technical illustrator in the report production department and I was a part-time reports editor. Actually, I was keeping an eye open for a permanent employment opportunity elsewhere that wouldn't shackle me to a desk or inhibit my predilection for adventure.

After an eleven-month courtship, Claire and I married in San Carlos, California, on May 17, 1969. Shortly thereafter, the Federal Bureau of Investigation accepted my application and we moved to Washington DC for fourteen weeks of basic training.

Living out of shabby apartments filled with moving boxes and anticipating the next transfer just months down the road didn't lend itself to acquiring a dog at the time; getting used to each other and dealing with the logistics and demands of a new profession presented challenges enough. But soon after we settled into an apartment in Tulsa, Oklahoma, in the spring of 1970, the urge to have a third party around the place struck us both simultaneously. Kids seemed out of the question for the time being, given the peripatetic nature of our lives.

Claire had grown up with a menagerie of tropical fish, turtles, dogs, and birds. I could not recall a time when I had not had a dog as a pal to romp with over hill and dale. The first decision having been made, we were faced with the second—which breed? We both were physically fit and loved the outdoors, so we started thumbing through dog books at the library to determine what breed would be best for an active, adventurous lifestyle. Most of the sporting breeds—goldens, pointers, labs, setters— were too big, as were the working breeds—huskies, Saint Bernards. We seriously studied basset hounds until we realized their low-slung undercarriages probably would get hung up on rocks, sticks, and other obstacles during our backpacking trips in the high country: not enough trail clearance. Besides, they tend to drool a lot.

After we sat down one day and compared notes about desirable characteristics, we decided we were looking for a purebred dog of medium size (thirty to forty pounds), with a

compact frame covered by a short coat (better flea and tick sur-
veillance and fewer shedding problems). The dog probably would
be a hunter or otherwise bred and suited for the outdoors. It
would have to be responsive, easily trained, and people oriented.

Then one Saturday we were studying a dog book we had
borrowed from the library. Nothing in the "A" section looked
interesting. "B" for basset was out. Then we paused at "Brittany"
and realized the research phase of the operation was over.

They used to be called Brittany spaniels. After the
American Kennel Club (AKC) accepted the fact that these
accomplished hunters from the French province of Brittany
were pointers, not flushers, they dropped the spaniel part of the
name in 1982. Now, at least in the United States, they carry the
title of Brittany. These sensitive, personable, agile, and indefatiga-
ble dogs are descended from a long line of bird hunters that
acquired an additional talent along the way—stealth and sub-
terfuge. It is said by some that in the province of Brittany,
French peasants used them to hunt game birds in the fields of
landed nobles, an illegal act in most jurisdictions. The distinctive
cinnamon and cream coloring of the dogs' coats helped the
poachers keep track of the dogs during their surreptitious forays.
The poachers also trained them not to bark—to be quiet so that
royal gamekeepers would not realize that plump pheasants, grouse,
and quail were being taken from right under their noses. Through
intentional genetic manipulation over years of breeding, the dogs'
gums became almost dry—perhaps so that they wouldn't run

around with incriminating feathers sticking to their muzzles.

Claire and I learned that to conform to AKC physical standards, Brittanys should be roughly square: from seventeen to twenty inches at the shoulder, with a body length of the same dimensions. In other words, the height at the shoulder should equal the length of the body. The most successful show dogs are thirty to forty pounds, with no tail or a tail cropped to no longer than four inches; and they have dense, flat, wavy coats of orange and white or liver and white.

Brittanys are equally at home in the house or the field, though anyone familiar with them at all knows they prefer the latter to the former. They crave interaction, whether it is with other dogs or humans. If they could talk (and thank the Lord ours can't), they would yammer constantly with entreaties to take them hunting or running, drive them around in a car with the windows open, include them in a gardening project (rototilling is good), play fetch with a bumper, talk to them— anything: just interact.

The five Brittanys we've lived with (I hesitate to say owned, because we're not certain who owns whom in these relationships) had personalities that were distinctive to a fascinating degree. The combination of field skills and people-friendly characteristics made them multi-dimensional animals that always challenged us, mostly positively, sometimes negatively. We came to cherish them not only as companions but also as links to wild canids—wolves, coyotes, foxes—those stealthy and graceful denizens of prairie and forest whose intelligence and innate cunning have allowed them to survive centuries of encroachment and outright assault by humankind. More importantly, our Brittanys served as partial substitutes for the children we were not destined to have. To this day, Claire refers to them as fur kids. As the years rolled by, we realized that they also served as passive mediators when we got sideways with each other—the infrequent serious disagreement that survived to the edge of dawn and threatened coexistence on into the day. These little guys sopped up ill feeling like benevolent sponges until there wasn't enough left to argue about. This, then, is the story of a man and a woman and their dogs—all Brittanys—and the joys and frustrations engendered by an experiment in interspecies cohabitation. Was the experiment successful? You be the judge.

Red

Training to become a federal law enforcement officer—which took place at the FBI Academy in Quantico, Virginia, and the Old Post Office and Department of Justice buildings on Pennsylvania Avenue in Washington DC—had taken most of the fall and slushy winter of 1969. After receiving our first offices of assignment, we forty-five newly minted G-men scattered like quail to places such as Indianapolis (the agent pronounced it Indian-No-Place), New York (moans of despair), and Cleveland (where the hell is Cleveland?). Packing our new brass badges, credentials, and Smith & Wesson .38 Special revolvers, we stuffed our meager belongings into our cars and hit the road.

In those days, a first-office agent routinely served for one year in a small field office under the tutelage of an experienced agent. Then the agency assigned him to a larger office for an indefinite duration. Accompanied by my wife, Claire, I went to Oklahoma City to serve my first three months. The northward tilt of most of the trees alongside the highway testifying to relentless winds was one of the first things we noticed the day we arrived in "Oak City." One evening in May, we were on our way home from a Neil Diamond concert when cascades of warm rain driven sideways by a massive thunderstorm obliterated our view of the road and forced us to pull over onto the shoulder until the storm passed overhead, rolling and tumbling in the black, strobe-lit sky.

We awoke the next morning to the wail of sirens and what appeared to be the aftermath of carpet bombing: homes blown apart and scattered across the ground; huge locust trees toppled and smashed; cars sitting in used car lots, windowless but otherwise unharmed; power poles leaning alternate ways, some broken off at the base and suspended from the lines. Five people died in the carnage, including a Baptist minister at a parsonage across the road from our office.

When my partner and I returned to my townhouse that morning for more film (the agency office had been damaged by the storm), we found Claire wrestling our double mattress down the hallway toward the bathroom. She had a tight grip on a small box that held what little jewelry she owned at the time. When I asked what she was doing, she replied, "I saw that funnel cloud out the window and thought it was headed this way. I heard that you should get in the bathtub and pull a mattress over you if a tornado is coming." (You have to understand that she was born in San Francisco and was in unfamiliar territory.)

"But where's the tornado?" I asked. We had just driven through most of the city and seen nothing but a drying sky.

"It was in that direction. Look. There's another one!" We looked out the sliding doors in the direction of the airport, and sure enough there it was—a cone of grayish jet exhaust spiraling downward from a departing aircraft.

In June 1970, I was reassigned to the Tulsa Resident Agency, a small satellite of the Oklahoma regional office, for the remainder of the first year. Tulsa was a welcome refuge from Oklahoma City's tornado-ravaged, wind-and-sun-blasted plain.

We found Red in the fall of that year. He was the last of a litter of seven born to a small nondescript bitch that appeared to want

little to do with him as he followed her around the backyard of a run-down ranch on Tulsa's southwest side. The rancher said the litter was AKC registered and we could have the last pup for $35. Red was only eight weeks old, so the rancher gave Claire a cardboard box for the trip home. As we drove back to Tulsa she held the box on her lap, looking at the bewildered little fuzz ball that gazed back at her with blue eyes. She was beginning to doubt that this was the right thing to do. "Having a puppy is a big responsibility," she mused. "They tie you down." But she seemed to be warming up to him. On the way, we stopped at the supermarket to buy him some food, a collar, a leash, and two bowls. Claire placed him on the sidewalk in front of the store and took a long look at him.

"Well, what do you think we should name him?" she asked, inspecting his distended belly that was crawling with fleas. I thought his name should have a provincial ring to it, so I suggested Sooner.

"Actually, I think those little red freckles make him look more like a Red. I'd like to name him Red." So Red he was, from that moment on.

His first checkup was a disaster.

"He has more fleas per square inch than any animal I've seen lately," the vet said, rubbing Red's fur the wrong way to reveal an army of tiny black spots scurrying for cover. "He also has a serious infestation of intestinal worms that are sucking him dry, so he's anemic. See, even his teeth are loose. You've got a sick puppy here. You'd better leave him with me for a while until I can tell how bad off he is. Where did you say you got him?"

As soon as we arrived home, we called the rancher and asked for an adjustment of the price, given the size of the bill we anticipated from the vet. He dug in his heels, reiterated his "as is" policy, and wouldn't budge. So we were forced to pay another $35 for a pup with fleas, worms, and loose teeth. The vet was so concerned about Red's condition that he spent the first night with him at the veterinary hospital. It took several weeks of treatment to build Red's health back to normal. When we came to take him home, the vet showed us a Dixie cup full of glistening, writhing intestinal worms—the buggers that had been cohabiting Red's pipes and sapping his strength.

Red began to burrow his way into Claire's heart using mischievous energy and humorous antics. One day Claire hosted a Tupperware party at our townhouse. After the guests had settled into the tiny living room and the Tupperware lady had launched her sales pitch, a low grinding noise—as if a giant termite was boring through the framing of the house—made the hairs on their forearms stand up like the spines on a saguaro cactus. Just as the Tupperware lady finished demonstrating the proper way to "burp" a plastic bowl, Red dropped the huge beef bone he'd been gnawing at the top of the stairs. Greasy with puppy saliva and fat, the softball-sized chunk bounded down the stairs making a series of loud thumps, coming to rest against the baseboard with a disgusting plop. Clearly annoyed at the distraction, the

Tupperware lady took one look at the glistening white bone festooned with shreds of meat and gristle and asked Claire, "Do you think we could put the puppy outside?"

Freed from the confines of the townhouse and the hypercritical Tupperware lady, Red got down to some serious puppy business; he chewed his way into a bag of barbecue charcoal on the patio. By the time Claire found him, having the time of his life tossing the briquettes in the air and spinning about in puppy abandon, he resembled a Labrador retriever—black from head to tail. The only remedy was to hose him off as best she could and then carry the little miscreant into the shower to scrub off the remainder of the lampblack.

As late fall turned to winter, cold fronts slid down across the Canadian border, searing the hardwood leaves crimson and gold. Early one morning after dropping me off at the Federal Building in downtown Tulsa, Claire and Red drove over to a pecan orchard that had advertised in the Tulsa Tribune: "Pick your own nuts, 59 cents a pound." For the next two hours, Claire stooped and stretched to gather scattered pecans off the ground, dropping the fat ones into a burlap bag that the orchard owner's wife had given her, and sliding Red along the ground after her in a cardboard box where he lay bundled in a blanket. The temperature was 27 degrees, with a light wind. When Claire appeared at the ranch house to settle up for the nuts, the rancher's wife took one look at her blue lips and clenched fingers, and hustled her inside by the fire. Both woman and pup were damn near as frozen as the glass-like panes of ice lying in irrigation ditches at the edges of the orchard. The rancher's wife insisted on serving Claire hot chocolate and giving a saucer of warm milk and a biscuit to Red. She refused to take any money for the nuts.

One morning while I was at work, Claire encountered a familiar denizen of the Oklahoma woods crawling along the curb near our townhouse—a box turtle. Box turtles live in hardwood forests and eat bugs and vegetation of all sorts. Their shells have a distinctive variegated yellow, black, and white pattern that helps them blend in with the forest floor. When they feel threatened, they let out a hiss and pull their legs and head inside the shell, then batten down the hatches by slamming shut a large flap in the front and small ones at each leg opening. Just so a car wouldn't turn the turtle into a Frisbee or what the comedian Jonathan Winters would call a sail turtle, Claire carried him to the small patio to the rear of our townhouse, dug him a little burrow in the cooler ground beneath a wooden box and left him some greens next to a water dish. She thought Bekins would be a good name for the latest addition to our growing menagerie.

After a few weeks, Bekins learned to trust Claire enough to come out of his burrow for food. When he saw the draperies opening in the morning, he scuttled over, raised himself up on the step, and begged for hamburger and greens, which she fed to him right out of her hand. At first, Red was curious about what must have appeared to him to be an ambulatory rock. He sniffed Bekins a few times, causing him to slam all the hatches shut.

Other than that, Red paid the turtle no mind. Bekins disappeared a few months later, never to be seen again. How he got out of the patio puzzles us to this day.

Merkin, the soft-shelled turtle, was another mystery to Red: a green hockey puck with legs that thrashed about tantalizingly whenever master or mistress took the thing out of its aquarium tank. In the wild, soft-shelled turtles grow as large as dinner plates. Ours was on its way, consuming prodigious amounts of turtle food, live crawdads, fish, snails—in fact, just about anything that fell into the tank. You might think that Red was getting a little nervous about spending all day alone in the same townhouse with this guy. Fortunately, a change in our lives forced us to find Merkin a loving home.

March of 1971 found us, like Willie Nelson, on the road again, northbound to Chicago for our next assignment, having no idea what the living conditions or work assignments would be like. We hit the outskirts of the city at rush hour and got sucked into the most horrendous, rudest maelstrom of traffic we had ever experienced. The Sheridan Surf, an old musty hotel not far from the shore of Lake Michigan, became our home for the next few months while we searched for permanent housing. Red was incarcerated at the Academy Pet Hospital in the near suburb of Evanston to the north.

While I worked downtown in the Loop, at the Everett Dirkson Federal Building, Claire roamed the crowded, brusque city looking for work. In between interviews, she visited Red at the kennel every day. A nondescript, beige-colored, one-story building, the kennel at first generated considerable angst. Claire's concerns evaporated after a few weeks when she arrived one day to pick up Red for a long walk along the shore of Lake Michigan and found him out of his cage, sitting on the sofa, while the veterinarian completed her paperwork. It was obvious Red had become the favored resident. During those lonely weeks before Claire was able to find a job, her romps with Red highlighted her days. She worked around the Sheridan Surf no-pet policy occasionally by smuggling Red into the hotel in a laundry basket. As luck would have it, on one such foray, several ladies entered the elevator on the ground floor. Up they went, chatting away, while the lump in Claire's basket lay there quiet as a field mouse, covered with underwear and shirts.

With both of us working, Red was alone in the town-house we had purchased near Richton Park, Illinois, thirty miles south of the Loop, from early in the morning until we returned home after six o'clock most evenings. Thus he became adept at using a corner of the basement we had lined with newspapers in case he had to relieve himself. This was our greatest transgression of rules in the Brittany Owner's Manual—leaving him without human contact for so long. In later years, after professional trainers had educated us more thoroughly about critical traits of the breed, we would paraphrase the television ad, "A Brittany Is a Terrible Thing to Waste."

Like most young field dogs left alone, Brittanys will find

things to entertain themselves. Their choices have nothing to do with cost, utility, style, fashion, or sentimental value. If it looks or feels interesting, it's fair game. For instance, one evening we returned home after another long day in Chicago to find the living room layered with fine down from a sheaf of cattails we had placed for decoration in an old milk can. Red had fetched them and systematically dismantled the fuzzy brown pods and stalks, leaving what looked like hurricane damage as far as we could see. A book titled *Learning Vietnamese* lay shredded next to the bookcase. I went ballistic, yelling at the dog and dragging him through the kitchen, then pushing him roughly down the stairs into the dark basement. I slammed the door and went back to help Claire clean up the mess, muttering all the while about out-of-control, untrained, mischievous, undisciplined dogs creating more work on top of all we had to do. My foul mood persisted through dinner and triggered a spirited exchange with Claire, who was more understanding about the pup's behavior than I was. "After all, he's only a few months old," she reminded me, "and alone in the townhouse all day. The energy has to go somewhere."

I was far less forgiving. The incident prompted me to reconsider our situation, even the notion of giving up the dog. Our back and forth caused deeper neuroses to surface: the petty details about her office colleagues that Claire lugged home every day, their foibles, the stupid way they dressed, their immaturity— banal gossip. I was guilty of insouciance, being too uptight about

my own job to notice her need for emotional intimacy. I was too focused on work and not enough on the family. Years later, I realized she was right—at the time I had not fully comprehended how day after day of stress was affecting my personality. Dealing with a demanding supervisor, a full caseload of interstate theft investigations, and adversarial encounters with truck hijackers; being hammered on the witness stand by defense attorneys; and preparing presentations before United States attorneys and grand juries had a corrosive effect on my disposition.

Just getting to and from work was a challenge. One winter evening the Illinois Central commuter train broke down a mile and a half from our townhouse, and we had to trudge through darkening cornfields crusted with snow: me in my wingtips and Claire in her calf-length leather boots. Early one October morning in 1972, a clerk raced over to my desk in the Dirkson Federal Office building and blurted, "There's been a crash on the Illinois Central at the 27th Street Station, and Claire hasn't shown up yet!" I grabbed keys to a squad car and drove south toward the scene of the wreck, red light flashing, siren wailing, and a huge lump in my throat. Badging my way through a Chicago police checkpoint, soon I was standing on a slight rise overlooking a scene of immense destruction. Several hundred yards away, one of the old-style commuter trains—olive drab cars built of heavy steel years ago—lay telescoped inside several of the more modern railcars that resembled aircraft fuselages: double-decker aluminum with large windows along the sides. A throng of passengers was staggering past the wreckage where bodies of some forty-five unfortunate victims lay mangled and twisted, some pressed against the glass windows like butterflies on display. Halfway down the column of surviving commuters, an umbrella was opening and closing in a kind of signal rhythm. I took a closer look and realized it was Claire trying to get my attention. She had seen me on the hill, wreathed in steam from a nearby utility pipe. The old lump in my throat returned big time until she was safely in my arms. Later that day, she would say I looked like one of the gods on Mount Olympus, come to pluck her from earthly misfortune.

But that night in the townhouse, the night of the strewn cattails, was one of the defining moments of our relationship. The discussion drifted away from the Brittany's misbehavior toward rougher waters—the nature of our relationship and its immediate future. I wondered: would this twelve-month-old union hold or fall apart at the seams because of significant differences in personality and constant stress from the brutal commute and exacting demands of the job? Claire seemed crestfallen, depressed, as she sat across from me at the dinner table. She had hoisted the squirmy puppy into her lap and was stroking his head. Wisely, we both declared time out to sleep on it. By the time the alarm clock sounded at 5:20 a.m. and we began to gird ourselves for another grinding day in the big city, we both had come to our senses; compared with serious dysfunctions in both our extended families, our marriage was far more precious, and worth preserving at all costs. This incident taught us to deal with internal and external stressors early and candidly throughout the relationship no matter what the genesis.

As the months with our first Brittany rolled by, we learned that, in addition to being field dogs, Brittanys are people dogs. They crave contact, especially when their humans conjure up exciting and challenging projects: canoe trips, bird hunting, running, cross-country skiing, bicycling, backpacking, long walks, skijoring, playing fetch. Mostly they are content just to be companions. Other times they are instigators. From Red we learned a lot about how Brittanys think—what impulses flash across their canine synapses—what turns them on and what sends them scurrying under the bed. One thing was obvious from the beginning: the promise of any outdoor excursion, no matter what the weather conditions, lights up a Brittany's nervous system like a floodlit space shuttle on the launch pad at Cape Canaveral. So whenever the opportunity presented itself, we struck out for wild country as an antidote to the griddle-flat sameness of the Illinois countryside. Just over the Minnesota line in Ontario, Canada, lies some of the wildest lake country in North America: Quetico Provincial Park has over a million acres of Canadian shield that glaciers bulldozed eons ago, leaving a canoe paradise, a mosaic of lakes stitched together by dense forests and sculptured bluffs. A cornucopia of scents and fragrances borne on a Canadian wind sweeping across mist-covered lakes, thrumming grouse and fluting loons, swirling rivers and snorting moose create a combination guaranteed to blow a Brittany's mind.

In September 1972, with Red in mind and our thirst for adventure and wild beauty whetted, we tooled on up the highway in our Volvo toward Ely, Minnesota, with the Brittany hanging out the window, cheeks ballooning in the slipstream. A few days later, our chartered Cessna 182 rose off the water with us, the pilot, and about two hundred pounds of gear, bound for an eight-day one-hundred-mile canoe traverse of Quetico Provincial Park. A Grumman aluminum canoe was lashed to one of the pontoons. Claire had squeezed into the rear seat with Red, a couple of backpacks, duffels, two paddles, fishing gear, and food bags. At full throttle in a steep climb over a patchwork of lakes, the Cessna was roaring and vibrating into the overcast sky. From the rear seat, Claire yelled over the engine noise, "He's wild! I'm not sure I can hold him." I looked back and saw that she had Red in a hammerlock while he struggled like a trapped wolverine toward the side window—eyes bulging, panting heavily.

When the Cessna reached altitude, the pilot throttled back and the plane leveled off, seeming almost to float compared to the grinding, shaking ascent from the lake. The rear seat became quiet. Then I heard Claire mumble, "I can't believe this dog." Later, after the pilot had dropped us off on the Canadian border and we had begun to paddle across the first of many wilderness lakes, she complained, "This dog of yours is something else." (He screwed up so he's my dog for the time being.) "As soon as the pilot throttled the engine back and the plane leveled off," she continued with a tone of disgust, "Red had a full body orgasm—all over my new jeans. Then he was okay. I think he really likes the trip so far."

After our Cessna air taxi shrank to a dot on the western horizon of Quetico Provincial Park and then disappeared completely along with its mosquito-like whine, it dawned on us we were truly on our own in the Canadian wilderness. For the next eight days we would have to find our way across a hundred miles of lakes and portages, dealing with weather, animals, the terrain, our own shortcomings, and mishaps as best we could. It would

be a team effort. For his part, the two-year-old Brittany would act as forward scout, sitting in the bow sandwiched between Claire's legs, watching for rocks or other obstacles to progress and taking note of the wildlife. Although useless as a deck hand, he was expected to haul his own gear over the portages in a pair of saddlebags Claire had sewn together for him out of surplus army gas-mask bags. After a few days he became so used to the routine that he would carry his pack up the trail out of sight, then meet us on the other side. Before long we began to find his pack lying in the sand on the far side of the portage, the precocious Brittany having learned how to throw it over his head.

These eight days became the stuff of Brittany dreams. Red reveled in the wash of scents and fragrances borne on breezes sweeping across the forests, lakes, and rivers. Like his brother the beaver, he paddled around the rocky shorelines of islands we had chosen for campsites. Once he dug such a gigantic hole at the base of a dead tree that we had to move our camp for fear of being crushed in the night by falling timber. During the planning stage, we had anticipated paddling across vast expanses of water and the brutal work of portaging; what we had not counted on was the ferocity of the weather. Fifty miles into the Quetico, we paused for a day on an island in Lake Kawnipi. These lines from my journal tell the story best:

> Having established a secure camp, we fish the shore farther on and I hook into a couple of eatable walleyes. We will have a good supper. We clean and fillet the three fish on the rock shelf at the north end of the island. Claire's northern is twenty-two inches long by the rule on my Silva compass. The walleyes are good eating size. The wonder dog trots over, sniffs around, and I pat his head with my fishy hand. He then bumbles into a yellow-jacket nest in the bushes near the tent. While defending himself against their efforts to colonize his head, he gets stung under the left eye. Claire plucks the stinger out, but for two hours he looks like a freckle-faced kid with a shiner. The firm white fillets are lying on a paper towel near the fireplace when the rain starts again, and this time it means business. We dive into the tent and listen to the loud drumming on the tight fabric. It's like being inside a bass drum while someone pours buckshot on it from twenty feet up. Confinement again. The smell of wet dog and

sweaty bodies. An incandescent flash bursts around us, followed about two seconds later by an ear-splitting slap of thunder. I'm reminded of incoming mortar fire in Vietnam: you're scared but there's nothing you can do about it, so you hunker down and endure. Through the rear window we can see the thick blue-black cumulonimbus tumbling and rolling in slow motion from the southwest.

The treetops on the far shore toss violently. Then the wind sweeps across our pitifully small island, sending the gunwales of the overturned canoe banging against the rocks, and waves slop-slopping against the shore. A few more half-hearted lightning bolts and the storm settles down into a steady downpour. I can see that Claire is worried again, although she is not saying much about it. Her main fear is that a stray lightning bolt will arc down and zap me, leaving her to somehow make her way back to civilization. She hasn't quite accepted the mood of this North Country yet, nor our distance from help should anything like that happen. The weather and the terrain are a threat to her now, rather than a challenge. Later on in the trip I will watch her change markedly.

To maintain our schedule to meet the pick-up van at the appointed time and place, we often had to paddle during storms. Fortunately, the Brittany had adapted to water travel, including heavy weather, like a seasoned sailor. During one such tempest in the middle of Lac la Croix, Claire was riding the bow like a wrangler. Sometimes a wave crest took her so high above the surface that her paddle stroke missed, so she paused until the canoe slammed down into the next trough and she could grab water. She was wet through from the rain and spray, but we both were pretty well acclimated to the elements after six days in lake country. The dog took it all in stride, sitting behind Claire's seat, peering out at me monk-like from beneath a rain tarp. When he leaned over the gunwale to catch a drink from time to time, I had to tell Claire to shift her weight to compensate. Never once did he get seasick.

We spent our last day paddling slowly, almost reluctantly, through the narrowing channel of the Nina Moose River toward the rendezvous point. Beavers, their industrious little hormones raging with the advent of fall, had constructed challenging wickerworks for us to negotiate. Where the river widened, we drifted through the stubble of wild rice harvested by Chippewa Indians. River otters playing hide-and-seek among the lily pads thumbed their noses at Red, who trembled with curiosity at their antics. As we pulled up to the last portage, the old adage that a canoe trip is the acid test of any marriage whispered in our ears. A hundred miles of portages, interminable windy lakes, thunderstorms, mosquitoes, freeze-dried food, and the occasional large mammal had both stressed and annealed our marital bonds. I looked at my bride of only three years with renewed fondness. "What a trooper for enduring all that with such grit and opti- mism," I thought to myself. "What a great sport." By carrying his share of the load, keeping a sharp vigil for roaming carnivores, entertaining us with his antics, and just being his gentlemanly self, the Brittany had added depth and dimension to the trip. His paw twitchings, mock running, and growling in his sleep after we arrived home proved to us that he was reviewing over and over the memories of his unbelievable adventure.

The intensity of commuting to the Loop and dealing with government attorneys, demanding supervisors, and complicated cases made weekends seem like treasured pockets of time to be savored as an inmate on death row would savor every minute. The basement of the townhouse often became my sanctuary from weather and the rough world; a place where, for example, I could do something as elemental as saw an old piece of wood we had found in the field. Regardless of what progress I had made on the project, Red would run down the stairs and bound over to me, leaping across the concrete floor, ears flopping, taunting me to take him outside. Depending on my mood, I would either scold him or lunge at him playfully. If the weather was bad, as it often was during winter months when cold winds from Canada swept down across the fields north of our complex, making the tawny grasses brittle and stiff as wire, I would continue working in the warm secluded confines of the basement, enjoying the sound of the sharp saw chiseling a neat kerf through the wood and the sweet odor of pine sawdust powdering the floor.

Even though he was not an especially assertive dog, Red's persistence often won out. I would place the tools in their proper receptacles above the workbench, sweep the sawdust into a neat pile, and throw it and the waste bits of wood into a hopper. These actions alone would excite him and he would dance even faster, bucking like an unbroken mustang and making "buff, buff, buff" sounds. But he was careful not to explode into a full bark because he knew that would bring a reprimand.

Our usual route was north from the townhouses along a gravel road that led to the Chicago and Joliet Railroad right-of-way. The tracks led west across a trestle to the field, which was flanked by a busy road on one side and housing developments on the other sides. Releasing Red, who had spent all day in the townhouse, from the leash was like launching a surface-to-air missile. From a sitting position, he would explode into a full run straight out into the field, diving into the deep grass as he might the ocean, and disappearing from view.

Often we would follow the serpentine wanderings of rabbit trails through the knee-high prairie grass until we reached a dry marsh. In the spring, the marsh was flooded and ducks paddled about, snapping at insects and plants. In the winter, the marsh was often dry, and I could stand at the lowest spot of the depression thinking it strange to be standing on ground normally flooded. The spiral shells of swamp snails dotted the frozen mud at my feet. Curious about how they renewed their species in the spring and what sort they were, I picked up a shell and peered into the opening. It was empty. It reminded me of a time five years earlier when my marine platoon participated in a training bivouac in the Philippines. Negrito guides led us into the jungle and taught us how to cut vines and drink the fresh sweet liquid that poured from the cut, explaining, "This is my water vine, Sir." They scrambled high into trees and picked ripe papayas, saying, "This is my papaya, Sir." They wove strong cords from bark and made snares for birds and small mammals. And they showed us how to catch frogs and snails, such as the one I held in my hand, and cook them in a section of green bamboo stuffed with rice and placed over a fire. When the rice boiled, we sucked the snails from their shells and ate them with the rice.

I enjoyed walking in the field, especially after a long week of working in the hubbub of downtown Chicago. I saw it as an unspoiled remnant of the prairie that the first pioneers considered a threat, something to come to grips with and defeat with plow and oxen, much as pioneers saw the eastern hardwood forests as something to clear with axe and bucksaw. And now I saw the same prairie as something to be preserved, a precious refuge from the surrounding conspiracy of asphalt and concrete. Obviously someone owned the field, but it was too marshy for building. Thus it remained unfenced and wild, a home for cottontail rabbits and red-winged blackbirds and, in the spring, mallard ducks, raccoons, and woodchucks. The dog was as necessary on these walks as a good pair of boots or a warm coat to ward off the probing winds. His mere presence was a comfort.

And watching him scamper across the field in search of wild game lent depth and dimension to the experience.

As spring approached, a warming southwest breeze often replaced the north wind. I could tell the direction of the wind by looking out the window at the American flag flying from a white pole near the community center of the townhouse complex we lived in. The southwest wind was welcomed because it lured insects and animals from their winter quarters. At night you could hear frogs in the marshes sounding for all the world like someone strumming a pocket comb with his thumb. Robins and blackbirds appeared in loose flocks, and mammals begin to stir in the field. But when the flag pointed southwest or west, we refrained from walking into the field. At those times, the flag warned us of a toxic wind blowing from the steel mills and oil refineries in Hammond, Gary, and East Chicago.

From our house I could not see the mills. But when the east wind blew, I knew they had come to us. It concerned me to know that with each breath outside, my lungs would lose a shade more pink and my heart would be forced to work a bit harder. I recalled a *Chicago Tribune* article, written by a physician, that carried three photographs: the lungs of a young child, those of a Chicago resident of twenty years, and those of a coal miner. The child's lungs were pink, I remembered, and those of the Chicagoan and the miner almost indistinguishably gray. So on those days of east wind, when the sun fell in orange panels on the white pavement, I stayed in the dark, cool sanctuary of the basement and worked in my workshop, hoping the wind soon would change. And on those days I ached for the montane landscape of the west, where the wind carried only pine pollen and the sweet fragrance of meadows and sedges warming in the alpine sun. Through those reveries I could almost smell the heavy vanilla scent exuded by Jeffrey pines high in the transition life zone of the High Sierra.

At times, the confines of the townhouse became enervating. Then we would stride purposefully north on the gravel road, with Red straining at the leash. As soon as the spring clip popped off his collar, he would race out into the brown field, tail erect, alert for the bobbing white forms of escaping rabbits. Although it was April, the north wind still carried a bite to it, so I raised the collar of my coat and buttoned the front. The gravel road ended at a double set of railroad tracks. I walked west on the cinders between the two sets of tracks, keeping one eye on Red, whom I could see flitting in and out of thorn bushes and weeds. I noticed with satisfaction that there were woodchuck dens in the dike paralleling the railroad right of way. As I watched, a rangy chuck flowed swiftly over the thawing ground through wild roses and disappeared into his burrow. But it struck me that soon the field south of there would be bulldozed and paved by the Intercontinental Development Corporation, which had built the house we lived in and a six-story apartment complex south of there, near the Illinois Central train station. The field would become a platform for yet another apartment building and the woodchucks would be driven out or killed. It saddened and infuriated me to think of the natural world retreating so precipitously before the uncompromising onslaught of concrete and steel. What was so untenable about the notion of green corridors and community buffers along streambeds and natural boundaries: places that would encourage animal propagation and migration from one wild area to another?

As we proceeded west, we crossed a steel railroad trestle, a viaduct over Crawford Avenue. I could feel as well as see the heavy Sunday traffic thudding beneath the iron girders. The sides of the bridge were splashed with blue and yellow paint, and someone, probably a high school kid, had written "Screw Crete" and "Rick and Sue." The north side of the bridge was emblazoned with "Rich Central." I walked beyond the bridge, whistled to the dog, and climbed down the north side of the bank. The dog, a hundred yards west of me, looked back at the whistle, then galloped to where I was crossing a wire fence into a cottonwood grove flooded with rainwater. Beyond lay fallow fields of rust and brown.

I sloshed after the dog through the cottonwoods and out beside an irrigation ditch swollen with water the color of light coffee. Some distance north of the ditch, we came to a runnel flowing in from the east. The ground to the south of the junction was low and ankle deep with rainwater and snowmelt. I winced as the icy water poured over the tops of my boots and pierced the sock warmth of my feet. I thought the hell with it as I watched the dog swim across the runnel. When I stepped across the ditch on a partly submerged log, it sank and my ankles turned to ice once again.

Once across, I hopped from hummock to hummock until the ground rose again and was comparatively dry. The clean smell of the wind surprised me until I remembered it was blowing from the northwest, not the northeast, source of infernal toxins. Dark veils of rain floated over, leaving a slate sky. I could see bright blades of infant grass beginning to emerge beneath the soggy remnants of last year's growth. We wandered north across the gently sloping field that had lain fallow for years, passing the crumbling carcass of a tractor, its rubber tires torn and burned by vandals, the shell of the body perforated by double-ought buckshot. A piece of farm machinery, the function of which was not apparent, lay beside the irrigation ditch, slowly dissolving in the rain, snow, and sun. I continued across the field, avoiding an occasional patch of thorns and low places where the water lay deeper than the height of my boots. With a windshield-wiper motion, the dog ranged within view, raising his head often above the grass to verify my direction. To the north, a single set of tracks ran east and west. In a flooded section below the south bank of this right of way, Red flushed a pair of mallards. They rose simultaneously from the water on frantic wing beats, so close I could see the iridescent green plumage of the male and the mottled field color of the female. The hues of her plumage mimicked the stalks of brown grasses in the field, as if a piece of the prairie was sailing across the sky. After they had gone, their tandem images floated in my mind's eye against the iron of the low sky, wings extended and necks parallel, one slightly above the other, as one would see a single frame in a sixteen-millimeter movie reel. It moved me to see wild ducks so close to home.

The rail bed was dry and level and the coarse cinders crunched under my boots, the rails themselves having rusted from disuse long ago. A small bridge made of creosoted ties led us west across a ravine; then we dropped down into the field again once safely across the low wet area. Passing through a grove of poplars, I saw that someone had hacked off a number of the smooth green trunks and laid them in a poor imitation of a log cabin. The stumps were knee high. It appeared as if whoever had cut and stacked them had long since lost interest in the cabin as a playhouse. Kids. I shook my head at the wastefulness of it all.

I whistled to Red and strode south from the faint road I could see proceeding into another grove of trees ahead, the wind pushing gently against my back. My feet, although wet, had warmed and were relatively comfortable. I crested a low hill, and ahead of me across a wide depression flooded with water stood another low hill crowned with trees still bare and not yet budding. As I walked across the field toward the rise, whistling occasionally to keep Red in close, I thought it might be prudent if I stayed with Second Squad in the trees behind me, directing cover fire as Third Squad advanced smartly in an open V formation. First Squad would be deployed to the right with every weapon trained on the grove of trees at the crest of the hill. If the enemy opened up on Third Squad before they reached the hill, I could deploy First Squad in a flanking maneuver, following in trace with Second Squad once they took the position.

Then I found myself on the hill, and the trees were close and dark. As I approached, Red flushed a cock pheasant that exploded out of the weeds at my feet, making my heart pound with surprise, primed for action as it was from my battleground flashback. The trees held a secret I had not anticipated. Among the wet trunks were scattered a water heater, a child's swing, a flattened bucket, and the shell of a gas stove. The faint traces of a crumbling foundation lay engulfed in weeds and wild rose. The discovery of the abandoned home site gave me an uneasy feeling, and I threaded my way beyond it down into a creek bottom among cottonwoods, crossing a rushing stream by balancing precariously across a thick branch.

A hollow filled with cane lay on the far side of the hill. Beyond that was lower ground with tan cattails swaying in the hurrying wind. Red was frozen, flat on the ground with his nose thrust beneath fallen canes and soggy cottonwood leaves. As I approached him, saying "steady, steady," in a low voice, he pounced and began wagging his stump of a tail furiously. I jerked him back by his collar and made him sit. Beneath the leaves, in a fist-sized hole lined with grayish fur, lay two infant rabbits. Their translucent ears were no larger than watermelon seeds and I could see that they had short baby fur. The commotion had excited them and they jumped convulsively within the nest, squeaking, eyes closed. After verifying that neither of the rabbits had been injured, I replaced the layer of wool that the dog had pulled away in his curiosity and gently tucked the rabbits back into the nest. Then we walked south to the tracks once again and followed the cinder rail bed east toward the townhouses I could see glowing orange in the lowering sun.

Late one June day, the townhouse once again felt confining. The dog and I walked out to the end of the gravel road and into the field. To the west, the low afternoon sun was glowing feebly through translucent stratus clouds that resembled mother of pearl. The nettlesome events of the day, a Monday, weighed heavily in my thoughts: Clark, the corrupt Illinois Central Railroad engineer, had outwitted one of our surveillances again, prompting a complete rethinking of our investigation plan. Grand Jury was scheduled for Thursday, and I had not yet prepared my testimony. All that faded before the panorama of the field. Saturated air from the Gulf of Mexico stifled even the bubbly melodies of red-wing blackbirds that clung like clothespins to the telephone wire paralleling the railroad tracks. Nothing in my field of view moved. Cottonwood and willow trees growing along the northern boundary of the field appeared bluish in the haze.

I followed the inquisitive, snuffling Brittany along a narrow path through luxurious weed growth, away from the noisy cinders of the rail bed. Wading into the tall grain-like grasses, clover, and purple blooming thistle, I experienced a sudden illusion of being submerged like a scuba diver gliding over coral and sand reefs festooned with seaweeds and other maritime vegetation, so thick was the humid air. Instead of striding across Illinois prairie, I imagined myself swimming through the aquamarine depths of some Caribbean sea. A sticky film of sweat rose on my forehead and neck.

The eager Brittany, tail wagging furiously, preceded me down a hard, narrow track that was no wider than eight or ten inches and had begun as a rabbit trail. Walking briskly behind him, I tried to keep up. Then I saw something that struck my heart like a cold draft: the chain-like tire treads of motorcycles weaving sinuously down the path, crushing nascent flowers and grasses, and leaving ruts filled with seep water. My spirits sank at the sight of the tracks; I had never seen them in the field before. The secret envelope of privacy I had enjoyed about this special sanctuary these past few months disintegrated.

As if cued into action by my thoughts, a motorcycle wheeled into view a hundred yards down the trail and bore down on us at considerable speed. The rider was a stocky teenager wearing shorts, tennis shoes, and a gray sweatshirt. Cocked back on his head was a white crash helmet with an opaque visor. Blue-white smoke blanketed the trail behind him, ejected by an exhaust system that had no muffler. Angered at the intrusion and its implications for a treasured refuge, I tore the heavy chain leash from around my neck and swung it in wide scythe-like arcs. The rider stopped, cranked the front wheel of his machine ninety-degrees, gunned the cycle, and tore off in the opposite direction, leaving a rooster tail of dirt and weeds drifting down through the plume of blue exhaust that marked his trajectory. As my anger subsided, it was replaced by a sense of loss. Even the Brittany seemed agitated and out of sorts. We both turned around and retraced our steps through the thick, humid afternoon toward home.

Some days Claire accompanied us on our walks into the field. She cherished Red and delighted in watching his ecstatic runs through the undulating field after his twelve-hour confine-ment indoors. She looked on him with a fondness very near that of a mother, reflecting the attention and care she alone had lavished on him through the trials of his puppyhood. As a result, the dog reacted warmly and affectionately toward Claire. And when he was injured, sick, or frightened, he turned more often to her for reassurance while reserving space for me as his field companion, leader of the pack, and roughhouse playmate.

One stifling Saturday in July, Claire and I returned alone from the field, filled with foreboding and concern because Red was missing. He had not responded to our calls at the turnaround point. The beginning of the walk had held portents of misfortune that should have been obvious: as we walked along the road near the townhouses with the Brittany on a short lead, speeding automobiles sent us scurrying for the gravelly shoulder more than once. We cursed the hurtling vehicles and mocked the occupants, who glared at us from dark, air-conditioned interiors. Beyond the road, I slipped the leash from the eager dog and watched him hurtle across the drying field. Nearby, teenage youngsters were tearing around their newly carved tracks on motorcycles, ripping the carpet of wild strawberries into divots that arced through the air. The flatulent noise banged against our ears. Thin ribbons of blue exhaust drifted over the field. Occasionally, one of the riders, seeing us, would gun his cycle, rear up on the back wheel, and speed down the widening track spewing dirt clods and shredded vegetation into the air. I cursed under my breath, called the dog to me, and leashed him until we gained the berm of the railroad tracks that would lead us away from the circus into the quiet meadows beyond the trestle. Looking back, Claire observed that the motorcyclists reminded her of chipmunks on an exercise wheel, spinning round and round the track with no apparent purpose other than the sensation of speed and racket. The din, like a hoard of angry hornets, was enervating. Red's nervousness disappeared when the leash came off his neck beyond the trestle, and he burrowed like a badger into the lush, weedy growth. Almost immediately, Claire ran toward the dog screaming his name. At first confused, I soon realized that she had heard or sensed a freight train coming along the tracks well before I had. After a few frantic rail-hopping, cinder-sliding moments, I grabbed the dog and pulled him down the embankment toward Claire just before the heavy tandem diesel electric locomotive thundered past, shaking the ground and hauling a hundred groaning, screeching, and hissing boxcars, flatcars, and tank cars west toward Joliet.

After the swaying caboose disappeared around the bend, I released Red and we followed him along the tracks to a path that led north past the rusting hulk of a farm tractor. The southwest breeze, flowing in waves, made the new grasses swirl and ripple. Compact-looking cumulus floated overhead in a milky blue sky. On the homeward leg, we realized we had not seen the dog for five minutes. Five minutes rolled into ten, then fifteen. We called, but got no response. The lethal tracks converged on the horizon. Red was nowhere to be seen. Sick with worry about the fate of the inexperienced dog, we walked east along the tracks past the cacophonous racket of the motorcycle track, crossed the trestle, and returned to the townhouse.

To our great relief, the Brittany returned home later that afternoon, somehow having traversed Crawford Avenue, the line of almost certain death. He was covered with burrs and dust, and his tongue hung down like a filthy rag. Claire speculated that the teenagers had herded him on their motorcycles along the dusty trails almost to exhaustion. Despite the softness of the day, I could not shake a growing feeling of inexorable encroachment, of shrinking natural refuge and loss of wild habitat with its intricate and delicately interwoven tapestry of plants and animals. I sensed a window in my mind gradually closing, leaving only the dispassionate, inanimate, the overdeveloped. It was time to move on.

matrix of diacritical marks, root verbs, leftward writing, and vocabulary called Arabic. Even with my background in French, Spanish, and Vietnamese, the learning curve was steep. More often than not, Claire watched the ten o'clock news alone while I plowed through homework assignments. Despite such linguistic stumbles as mixing up the Arabic "banadura" (tomato) for "bunduqiya" (rifle) so that my sentence came out "The soldier carries a tomato on his shoulder," graduation day finally rolled around, and Despina awarded me an honors certificate. Even more exciting to Claire was the news that we would be assigned to the counter-terrorism squad at the FBI field office in San Francisco.

By stretching our finances to the limit, we bought a home in Mill Valley, a village north of the Golden Gate Bridge that is tucked into redwood groves at the foot of 2,500-foot-high Mount Tamalpais. A web of trails traversing the mountain lay practically in our backyard. Beckoning over the western horizon were fog-washed hills and the Pacific Ocean; to the east lay the gold country, and beyond that, high Sierra wilderness. Neither we nor the rambunctious Brittany could believe our good fortune.

It took me several weekends to frame a ten-foot-square "condo" in the basement of our house so Red would be comfortable alone during the workweek. The finished enclosure featured an insulated kennel, carpeted surfaces, classical music, plenty of water and chew bones, and a hatch that opened to a terraced yard with views of the distant hills. Red now enjoyed the best of worlds we could offer—both inside and out.

Red's personality quirks were a great source of amusement. For example, he loved ice cream. He had learned to associate the words "ice cream" with the sweet, frosty, dairy treat humans know and love, a treat that is not on a hunting dog's training table. Nevertheless, you could count on Red sitting next to you when you opened the freezer door for an after-dinner treat. Once in a while, if an offer to share didn't come soon enough, he took matters into his own paws.

It is possible that Red's fondness for ice cream segued somehow into a fascination with cross-country ski trips—that he saw the spring snowfields of the Sierra Nevada as one humongous ice cream sundae to be consumed in small nibbles or, failing that, just to slide across on his belly or roll about in like an ecstatic river otter. We regularly indulged his passion by taking him along on three- to four-day sojourns into Desolation Wilderness or the Carson Iceberg near Ebbett's Pass. Claire, anticipating his discomfort regardless of the Brittany's reputation for toughness, sewed him a parka covered in Gore-Tex, lined with Buchanan plaid wool, and filled with polyester fiber insulation. Since he was warm enough on the trail, he wore it only in camp after the sun had drifted into the trees and the temperature dropped. At night he slept in our tent on an Ensolite pad. For a domesticated animal, Red showed some impressive backcountry ingenuity. If the snow was new and deep and wouldn't support his weight, he would follow us, using our ski track as a pathway, sometimes trying to catch a free ride on the tails of Claire's skis.

On the first few trips, Claire's fear of turning into a popsicle at night when the temperature dropped below freezing prompted her to build huge fires. This was okay by the Brittany, who watched her drag tarp loads of dead sticks into camp until she had created a structure rivaling the Stanford bonfire. Touching it off with a match after supper was akin to watching the back end of the space shuttle light up during launch sequence—a cone of flame ten feet high. Consequently, we all stood back about twelve feet, watching our steaming trouser legs like hawks. For Claire's benefit, I recounted the old North American Indian adage, "White man build large fire, stand far away; Indian build small fire, stand very close," but it didn't make any difference. Shuffling around in the dark for a post-bedtime pee, you had to be careful that you didn't do a header into the six-foot crater the fire had melted in the snow.

On one spring trip into the Ebbett's Pass area of the Sierra Nevada Mountains, Red was tucked comfortably into his corner of the tent, just fading into a deep sleep induced by the thin air and miles of travel. I was stepping into the doorway of the tent when I turned for a moment to admire the crystalline geometry of Orion, the Gemini, Canis, and Taurus marching westward against a backdrop of infinite space. Suddenly, a phosphorescent streak ripped a seam in the sky from west to east, trailing sparks and roaring toward the northeastern horizon. I yelled something about a huge meteorite falling into the far side of the lake. Before the others in the party could react, it was gone. We later found that not only my estimate of its trajectory and distance but the very nature of the object was off by many orders of magnitude; it turned out to be a Russian satellite that fell into Saskatchewan.

Red's last foray into the snowy mountains was bittersweet. Our five-mile route north of Carson Pass one March day climbed to a saddle, then dropped over into the Upper Truckee Valley. A brief snowstorm had covered the classic base of corn snow with three inches of fluff that balled up in the Brittany's feet and tired him out so much that he sat down in the ski tracks a quarter mile short of base camp. We had never seen him just give up like that before. Claire took his pack and removed ice balls from his pads and beneath his chest so he could move on down the groove. Soon he was curled up in his parka on top of my sleeping bag like a Douglas squirrel in a hollow tree. Though he easily kept pace with us during our reconnaissance tours the next day and on the trip back to Carson Pass, we were distressed to see that he was slowing down.

But slowing down is all relative to a Brittany's energy level. Red was eleven years old when Claire and I attempted to climb Mount Shasta in Northern California by means of the southern route. At 12,800 feet, the Red Banks, a band of volcanic conglomerate more than fifty feet high, stopped us cold. We had been on the mountain for better than five hours, trudging all the way from Horse Camp at 7,500 feet. We were out of water. The 14,162-foot summit appeared deceptively close, but in fact was at least a couple of hours away. Red collapsed in a pile of dusty fur, and we accepted the agony of defeat.

At his advanced age, summer backpacking trips were more to his liking than the harsh, Mars-like terrain of glaciated Pacific volcanoes. He readily assumed the role of point man, trotting along the trail ahead of the party, on alert for other hikers or dangerous predators. But Red addressed his sentinel duties selectively, according to the perceived threat, his current comfort zone, and the anticipated blowback. A good example occurred one night during a late summer foray into the Mokelumne Wilderness southwest of Carson Pass. A grunting, snorting, and branch-snapping something crashing through the woods just east of our camp on Long Lake jolted Claire and me straight up in our sleeping bags. Headlines pulsed through my cobwebbed brain: SASQUATCH TRASHES WEEKEND CAMPERS. After a few minutes, a palpable quiet enveloped us. The constellation Scorpius continued its westward course. The Brittany tucked between our sleeping bags faked a long drawn-out snore as if to say, "I'm asleep, couldn't hear a thing, therefore don't have to do my canine duty and bark or chase whatever that big, scary thing out there is." The following day while threading our way through thick lodgepole timber toward the trailhead, we found the evidence that confirmed the identity of our night visitor— the unmistakable prints of a young black bear.

Aware of the requirement to keep a Brittany constantly challenged with new adventures, we decided to explore some real estate only diehard backpackers bother to visit. Like a displaced chunk of the Cascade Mountains, the Yolla Bolly Middle Eel Wilderness rises 7,200 feet up out of a hot rocky plateau thirty miles west of Red Bluff, California. Its anomalous weirdness includes vegetation that reminds you of the mountains around Grants Pass, Oregon—Douglas Fir, Pacific yew, salal, Oregon grape. The smallish lakes are cratered into the sides of broad volcanic ridges that rise up like pyramids from the sands of Giza, holding snow on the lee sides into early summer. Curious about the reputed lair of Sasquatch, and as a favor to Red, who at the age of twelve didn't have many such trips left in him, Claire and I visited the Yolla Bolly.

For two days we rambled through the expansive meadows, climbed volcanic outcroppings to view the lights of Red Bluff twinkling in the twilight, and scrambled across rocky ridges with the aging Brittany. Red seemed to savor each hour, pausing often to sample the wind or poke around the sedges at the edge of a pond. He was beyond the stage in his life where the optimum thrill was tearing through the country like a wild coyote. For once, his measured pace matched ours; but we had to make allowances for his failing faculties. On the second day, we were climbing the north side of a steep ridge timbered with Douglas fir when we suddenly realized we hadn't seen Red for a few minutes. After a quarter hour of calling his name, we started a grid search. Soon we spotted him sitting alone in a sunlit clearing, gazing downhill, oblivious to our presence. It was almost as if he knew he was lost and couldn't hear us, but believed we would rescue him sooner or later if he stayed in one spot.

After supper at our lakeside camp, we tucked into our small mountaineering tent. Red settled in next to us in a lean-to affair improvised out of a small tarp. Just past midnight, a weak cold front drifted over, dropping light rain. When I peered outside the tent to check on Red, I discovered he was gone. By following the cord we had tied him to, I located him on the slope below us sitting quietly in the rain near a rhododendron bush, ears flapping in the light breeze. He was watching tendrils of mist curl through the treetops, and seemed to be savoring subtle fragrances borne on the freshening breeze. It was as if he knew he would be leaving soon, and wanted to savor every minute, even if they were soggy. I sat with my arm around him for a while in the light rain, enjoying the closeness and companionship of this remarkably loyal animal and our common passion for wild places.

During Red's annual physical in the summer of 1982, our vet diagnosed a mild heart murmur for which he prescribed Lasix. Surprisingly, at age twelve, Red still forged ahead on the leash as if he was hot on the trail of an escaping ring-necked pheasant. His pace through the neighborhood and on the trails was exhausting. No doubt Claire's homemade dog stew had something to do with his energy level. But his tough constitution masked an even greater threat to his health.

One evening almost a year later, after he finished his dinner, he started panting heavily and showed signs of distress— as if he might throw up. I ushered him down to the backyard where he continued panting and started heaving. Then he collapsed. Alarmed by what appeared to be signs of considerable pain, I carried him back into the house. In fifteen minutes we arrived at the emergency veterinary clinic beside the freeway in Terra Linda. A preliminary X-ray revealed a mass in Red's abdomen. The attending vet recommended a thorough exam by our personal veterinarian. A few days later at Madera Pet

Hospital, X-rays glowing on the light wall told a grim story. Dr. Gary Jones confirmed to Claire that the mass in Red's abdomen might be malignant and did not look operable, but that he could tell more during an exploratory operation in two weeks. In the interim, she should take him home and make him as comfortable as possible.

True to the existential way he had lived his life, Old Man Red savored those two weeks, lounging in his favorite bed in the closet, and relishing special meals Claire prepared for him from scratch and the extra attention we gave him. May 19, 1983, the day I drove Red to the veterinary hospital for his operation, was one of the most beautiful spring days that ever had graced our home in Mill Valley. Before getting in the truck, we took a walk together down by Salt Creek, savoring the early morning sun— the way it slanted obliquely through the dewy oat grass, igniting poppy blossoms, lupines, and funnel-shaped spider webs. A spring breeze, redolent with bay laurel, damp oak leaves, and the astrin- gent odor of tarweed, puffed through the trees. This smorgasbord of scent amplified by the dewy ground energized Red's bird-dog genes, sending him snuffing and snorfling through the grass, tail wagging. We drove slowly up the freeway to Madera Pet Hospital, and I handed him over to the attendant on a cheap nylon lead that she had given me. Then I watched him saunter down the corridor, pause briefly to exchange tail wags with a Jack Russell, and disappear around the corner. On the drive back down Highway 101 toward the bus pad where I would catch a number 80 to the Federal Building in San Francisco, I kept telling myself that Red would be fine. Dr. Jones would declare the tumor benign, he would remove it, and in a few days we would take Red home to recover. But the little voice in the recesses of my mind, the same one that whispered so darkly when we loaded my best squad leader, Sgt. Dawson, on the helicopter in Viet Nam after a 7.62 mm NATO round traveling twelve hundred feet per second had torn into his chest at close range and I had whispered, "Hang in there, Sgt. Dawson, you'll be okay," was muttering again like the melody of a pop tune rattling around inside my head. Sure enough, that afternoon Claire called me at the office in tears. The tumor was malignant and inoperable; she had given Dr. Jones permission to put Red down. I met her at the curb outside the Federal Building, and we drove north across the Golden Gate Bridge and over the Waldo Grade toward home. I sat in the passenger seat silent, locked up, wondering how in the world Claire could manage to rattle on about such an epic tragedy even though her voice was quavering and cracking. All I could manage to say was, "Yeah. Yep. He sure was."

When our neighbor Barbara Scafidi strolled out to the end of her driveway to inquire about Red's condition, Claire was the one who gave her the bad news. As for me, I was so mute with grief I couldn't utter a word, couldn't even say "Hi." The hardest part of letting go after thirteen years of Red's gentle company was packing up his gear that afternoon. Despite a paralyzing sense of loss, Claire, the practical Virgo, insisted on getting rid of his blankets, his toys, his bowls, and other reminders of his absence. That final chore done, Claire and I jumped on our bikes and pumped furiously down the trace of the old Northwestern Pacific Railway toward Sausalito, letting the wind blowing off a fog bank in Tamalpais Valley wash over us and dull the pain somewhat. For months, Red's death lingered as a dull ache and an acute sense that the third member of our pack of three was gone forever. We miss him to this day.

Max
Maximillian of Marin

After Red's death from abdominal cancer in 1983, two years rolled by before Claire could even think of looking for another dog. But as time passed, she realized that searching for another canine companion soothed the heartache somewhat, even though she knew she could never replace Red. We haunted dog shows, drawn inexorably to the Brittany benches where we engaged the owners in lengthy discussions about bloodlines and characteristics and personalities. Running her hands across the silky fur of Brittany puppies and veteran show dogs served as a soothing tonic for the empty chamber in Claire's heart. Once she called me from Salinas, a two-hour drive to the south, where she'd found a likely litter. But none of the pups spoke to her or plucked at her heartstrings.

One day after work we drove to Novato to check out a litter advertised in the local newspaper. As we sat in the kitchen of a modest tract house, the breeder opened a kiddie gate and fourteen puppies scampered into the room. Claire seemed almost disinterested, tired of the searching. I caught and held a husky male with an overlarge head and big feet. His coat was rich and thick and about evenly divided between cinnamon and white. His breath smelled of heavy cream.

"Feisty little guy, isn't he?" I asked. "What do you think?"

Two hundred dollars got us out the door with the pup, as we would call him for the next few weeks while searching for an appropriate name. Little did we suspect that we had introduced into our home a canine version of Dennis the Menace, a hard-headed, assertive, rambunctious, energetic Brittany as different from Old Man Red as Dennis Rodman is from Charles Osgood. Claire decided to call him Maximillian of Marin, or simply Max, one of the most shopworn names in dogdom.

Thus began an intense struggle for primacy. When he realized that I would not be intimidated into accepting the number two slot in the pack, Max started in on Claire. After a particularly bad evening of being bitten on the ankles, ambushed, and chased in and out of rooms while she tried to do her chores, Claire broke down. Through her tears she swore, "No, damn it, I'm not going to let him get the better of me. I'm going to see this through if it kills me. Or him. Anybody but us would have hauled him to the pound by now."

As Max matured, we began to realize we owned an alpha dog. Our first obedience instructor confirmed it after pinning him upside down on the asphalt of a basketball court by the scruff of his neck while Max struggled and squealed in outrage. Although it pained us to do it, we obeyed her instructions to repeat the same procedure at home every time he tried to dominate us, until he got the idea he was bottom, not top dog.

We took Max through three formal obedience classes, noticing gradual improvement each time. That he would never achieve the dog trainers' designation of CDX (companion dog expert) also became apparent. One night while trying his best to comply with the "sit-stay" command in a line of twelve student dogs arrayed across the basketball gymnasium in Greenbrae, nine-month-old Max broke ranks, succumbing to the seductive fragrance of Nikko, a two-year-old Gordon setter wearing a red bandanna around her neck. To the silent amusement of the rest of the class, I made the long walk over to where Max was

FIRST IN
GROUP

SIR FRANCIS DRAKE
KENNEL CLUB
• SUMMER 1984
VICKY
FOX & COOK

enthusiastically trying to force his affections on her, pulled him off, and placed him in the penalty box.

Show judges loved him, or maybe it was the naïve way Claire trotted around the ring wearing white shorts, Max biting the leash or stopping to drop a load, which I, like a rodeo clown, would then have to scoop up. As a puppy, Max won several ribbons. But he never seemed to enjoy waiting for the next event, surrounded by sweating, overwrought people and nervous dogs.

When he was three months old, we took Max on his first backpacking adventure into the Desolation Wilderness of the High Sierra Mountains with Sally and Ray, our occasional trail companions. It was no surprise to see the montane environment ignite his bird-dog genes, even at that young age. Bouncing out of the trailhead, he inhaled the alpine air in great gulps, scampered through forest duff, and pounced cat-like on the first snow patches. A cornucopia of sights and smells overloaded his system. Soon after we made camp at a lovely alpine tarn called Tyler Lake, he fell asleep in Claire's lap, looking for all the world like a stuffed animal. By the following day, she had forgiven him for chewing a neat hole in her new backpack, boring like a ravenous badger right through a layer of Cordura and paper plates to get at ripe bananas. For some reason, he loved bananas. (A friend who house sat while we were on the East Coast for a week one fall discovered this obsession after finding on the kitchen floor evidence of what he termed "the great banana massacre of 1986.")

When night engulfed our tent, small sounds beyond our range of hearing tantalized him: field mice skittering across logs, birds flitting through hemlock trees, even beetles scuttling along the granite. He popped up and down like a jack-in-the-box for twenty minutes until I stuffed him in the space between our sleeping bags and he passed out. Early the next morning, he came scooting down a rib of granite from the direction of our companions' tent, carrying Sally's panties in his mouth. Later he took off with Ray's knit cap. When we caught him, we discovered he had chewed a hole in it. Claire's nurturing genes assured his comfort and safety on these expeditions: he inherited Red's homemade blue Gore-Tex parka stuffed with fiberfill and lined with wool, a navy blue Gore-Tex raincoat, rubber hunting boots, and nylon saddlebags.

During the workweek, Max lived in our backyard in a blue plastic 55-gallon drum that once held caramel syrup. He was perfectly happy there, eyeballing the pedestrians and dogs walking along Underhill Road and stalking bugs, birds, or Stumpy, the alligator lizard that lived in the ground cover at the bottom of the hill and had lost part of his tail in an encounter with the inquisitive dog. But as aggressive and independent as Max was, he still seemed to require a certain minimum of human interaction. Although we had trained him to pass his days quietly in the backyard, when we arrived home from work each day, he would rush into the house and throw all forty-six pounds of muscle and bone into Claire with an exuberance worthy of a high school football player. He insisted on sitting up on his haunches, wrapping both paws tightly around her wrists, and, in warbling whines and groans, telling her about his day. By the sound of it, some days were worse than others.

That he was an active, inquisitive dog became apparent almost immediately after he entered our home as a puppy. One bad habit we despaired of breaking was raiding Claire's purse for the Big Red chewing gum she keeps in it. Loud admonishments in the form of firm commands, water squirted from a bottle, or, eventually, hysterical screaming had no effect; almost every night Claire would find her purse on the bedroom floor amid scattered makeup, checkbook, Kleenex and—Big Red wrappers. After several months of this foolishness, she'd had enough. Just before dinner, she set a small mousetrap, laid it carefully just inside her purse, and went back to making dinner. Fifteen minutes later, we heard a loud snap and a "*Yipe!*" and watched Max scoot out of the bedroom at warp speed and head straight for the safety of his "fort" beneath the lamp table in the corner of the living room. From that moment on, Claire had all the Big Red to herself.

Fortunately, the curiosity and energy eventually metamorphosed into more responsible behavior as Max matured. The occurrence of shattered planters, scattered handbags, shredded clothing, and other minor disasters tapered off. He settled into a routine of more or less responsible activism, challenging us to play by standing at the kitchen door with a stuffed pheasant toy in his mouth, growling and prancing provocatively. But from time to time his innate exuberance still erupted spontaneously. During one of my out-of-state assignments, Claire was watching television in the living room after dinner, sipping the last of her cabernet. For some unfathomable canine reason, Max launched himself from the far reaches of the room without warning and slammed into her, sending the cabernet shooting upward in a purple geyser that mushroomed at the apex of its arc and descended in a shower that saturated a considerable radius of the carpet, not to mention Claire, the chair she was sitting in, and the dog.

Another way Max burned off excess energy was to wad up a blanket in his paws, clamp it in his jaws, and slip into a kind of trance, lying down with his eyes rolled back and pumping his paws like a puppy suckling its mother. When Claire asked about it, the veterinarian guessed Max might have been taken from his mother too soon. Nonetheless, he seemed calmer after a good "nurse." As Brittanys go, he was bigger than the norm. Twenty-one and a half inches at the shoulder and twenty-one inches long, he weighed forty-six pounds at full maturity. Clearly, he was off the AKC charts for show competition. His coat was a patchwork of rich cinnamon alternating with ivory on his underbelly and legs. A thin ivory flame illuminated his forehead. His overlarge head was a consequence of being a Maxwell, according to Dave Saucerman, the bird dog trainer in Fairfield who was referring to our dog's blood tie to kennels operated by Marilyn Maxwell in Montara, California. He'd never really grown into his big feet like most field dogs. Not until we had to order a medium pair of rubber hunting boots for his rear paws and a large pair for the front paws did we realize the extent of his asymmetry.

Max had little personality quirks that endeared him to us. If you ignored his entreaties to play, he'd grab a favorite toy and throw a tackle on you as you tried to escape. That routine evolved into wrestling sessions between Max and me (usually initiated by the Brittany). The early encounters were painful; Max's sharp puppy teeth threatened to shred not only my hide but the clothes I was wearing. The solution was for me to train Max to select a rubber toy from his toy box before engaging in a roughhouse session. Only after Max obeyed my command to "get your mouth guard" could the match begin.

As aggressive and headstrong as he was, Max sometimes showed us what an interdependent component in this pack of three he had become. One spring I made the mistake of letting him watch my preparations for a cross-country ski trip to the backcountry of the High Sierras with some buds. Like a referee at a tennis match, he watched me sort out the tent, sleeping bag, boots, skis, poles, navigation gear, clothing, and food. Claire informed me later that the evening I left, he refused to eat his dinner. A serious case of separation anxiety had struck. He moped around the house for days until his appetite finally returned. Other behavior prompted mirror actions. For example, after watching me quaff a glass of water before a hard run in the hills, he would walk over to his water bowl and do the same— tanking up. In the morning, he would wait politely until I was seated and well into my Raisin Bran before diving into his kibble.

But the field triggered primal instincts in him. The musky scent of deer and pheasant, quail and dove, the acrid fragrance of wet oat grass and the salt marshes of the North Bay were catalysts that drove him like a restless spirit across open ground in search of the quarry his genes were telling him to find. Try to hug him or pet him in the field and he'd likely ignore you, preoccupied as his mind was with scanning that hedgerow or brushy ravine he'd not yet covered. Dave, the trainer, thought he had potential as a field trial champion. "Judges love them big runnin' dogs," he said one overcast day at the Suisun Marsh Hunting Preserve. "And that's what you got there, a big runnin' dog. I run him this morning four times already and look at him." Max was racing across a flooded rice field to investigate a tree line near a canal, dragging thirty feet of wet, dirty rope behind him.

We left Max with Dave one September while we vacationed in North Carolina. For a few weeks, Max would hone his skills on live birds with a trainer who knew him and his littermates, the eccentricities of his bloodline. Claire pictured him pining away in his cage, wondering where we were, possibly escaping to find his way home. More than once I told her not to worry, saying, "Dave is a professional and Max will go into his bird dog mode." Nothing helped—still she worried. The day we returned and went to check on his progress, a chilly wind swept the marshes. In the distance we saw a man, a dark-colored dog, and what appeared to be Max, inbound at an easy canter. He

loped into the parking lot dragging a filthy rope and jumped up on Claire, smearing her white slacks with marsh mud. Then he trotted off to compare notes with the slender little female short-hair Dave had paired him up with that day. Our absence hadn't fazed him one bit.

The day we finally gave up on field trials was longer coming than it should have been. Sheets of cold rain swept Grizzly Island, a hunting preserve at the northern apex of the Sacramento River delta. It was one of the first heavy storms of the fall season. Hunters, horses, and dogs hunkered under what overhead shelter there was around a complex of trailers and box-like office buildings, while runnels of rain poured off the roofs. Stubble rose up out of the flooded fields like hair on a hog's back.

After what seemed like an interminable wait, the judges for the "Derby run" called for Maximillian of Marin. I almost missed the announcement, so unaccustomed was I to the official name Claire had chosen for Max when she registered him with the AKC.

Max was paired with a wiry little Brittany that looked very experienced. I mounted a solid-looking bay mare and my competitor swung up onto a white gelding. Two elderly judges on black horses followed us as we jockeyed for position at the starting line. The gun sounded and the dogs raced out through the flooded fields, throwing fans of muddy water before them. Soon they were one hundred yards ahead, beginning to track back and forth through the soggy stubble, settling down, search-ing for traces of scent. At the corner of the course, where the party was to turn left and parallel a levee, my competitor's dog bolted and shot straight north, ignoring his owner's frantic yelling. After a few minutes, the judges told the man, "Go recover your dog, sir," and instructed me to continue along the course with Max, who had heeded my command to "hup" to the left. The hunting gods were smiling so far.

We made another ninety-degree turn and soon entered a flooded paddy. Rain squalls swept across the soggy terrain. Max's ecstatic leaps produced impressive sprays of water that flushed a bedraggled chukar from beneath a bush. He scrambled to catch the bird as it zigged and zagged through the field. Tiring of this adolescent display, the judges intoned, "Sir, recover your dog." As I started to dismount, my horse stepped into a ground squirrel

burrow on the side of a levee dike and her hindquarters collapsed. I slithered off her back, turned her over to a handler, and
walked back to the ranch building with Max in tow. Both of us
were soaked through to the marrow and beginning to feel the
chill. Even though I thought Max had acquitted himself well for
a young dog, the derby prizes went to dogs that had been trained
by professionals.

Brittanys needn't be restricted to hunting fields and show
rings. With a little cross training, they even can become decent
mountaineers, as our three tries for the summit of Mount Shasta
in five years testify. On our first attempt, Claire and I naively
thought we could waltz up the south route (the one experienced
mountaineers call the tourist route) in one day from Horse
Camp, wearing shorts, carrying a bag lunch and one bottle of
water. That was the time Red, at age eleven, had collapsed with
exhaustion. After we lost Red to abdominal cancer, we missed

his exuberant company on outdoor treks. So at breakfast one day I suggested to Claire, "Let's climb Shasta for Old Man Red. He would appreciate the gesture." Subtle psychology at work here. From that moment on, Mount Shasta became a personal challenge. It would serve as a sepulcher for Red's ashes—a fitting memorial to his stamina, his loyalty, his zest for life. All we had to do was reach the summit before we both got too old or the damn thing exploded like Mount St. Helens.

On our second pilgrimage up the south side route, Max nearly trashed himself and gave us heart attacks when he almost fell off the mountain. Our climbing party had strapped on crampons, hoisted packs, and were getting ready for the ascent when we heard shusha, shusha, shusha out across the icy ravine. It didn't sound like anything we had heard before in the mountains. Then we spotted Max, who had decided to start for the summit on his own. Wearing his rubber hunting boots, he had worked his way out to a steep section, started to slide, and then maintained his position by frantically spinning his wheels. That was the shusha, shusha sound. I rushed out to save him before he ran out of gas and slid all the way back down to the trailhead several miles away. Our ill-fated attempt ended 162 feet short of the true summit in an arctic wind. We turned blue with cold and altitude sickness. Accepting the agony of another defeat, we slithered downhill on our butts, plowing neat grooves through the slushy corn snow. At home we discovered that Max, only a year old and a new trail companion at the time, had sustained painful solar burns on his—how do I say this politely?—undercarriage. On the next trip, since Max is her dog, Claire would apply zinc oxide to the sensitive parts, thus avoiding a condition described by Jerry Lee Lewis when he sang, "Goodness gracious, great balls of fire."

One afternoon during that third trip, a year or so later, Max, Claire, and I found ourselves on the north slopes of Mount Shasta in northern California as a distant concussion reverberated through stunted lodgepole pines. We were huddled near a boulder complex at timberline, plotting our next move. To the north, thunderheads dragging veils of rain before a capricious breeze bore down on us. We gazed up at tilted slopes of the 14,162-foot volcanic cone, calculating the distance along the Hotlam-Bolam Ridge to our objective for the day, a bivouac at 11,000 feet. In between lay a corridor of ice and snow flanked by tapering walls bulldozed by glaciers eons ago: no shelter, no protection should a stray lightning bolt arc down from dark cumulus. Claire was not amused by the light and sound show.

"Was that lightning? Maybe we should just camp here instead of moving up any farther," she said, cinching the hood of her anorak tightly around her face. After nineteen years of marriage, I still couldn't decide whom she resembled most; sometimes her dark features reminded me of the actress Ali McGraw—or, when we got sideways with each other, Popeye's girlfriend Olive Oyl. Over the years, Claire has maintained a rigorous exercise regimen that's kept her frame so thin and strong that even in middle age she leaves me in the dust on most wilderness excursions.

But before we left the trailhead that day she cautioned, "Don't tell me how much I'm carrying this time. I don't want to know." Even though thirty-three pounds of food and equipment in her custom-fitted pack with high-tech suspension and an internal frame would bruise her hips and clavicles by the end of the trip, she wouldn't say a word about it.

Mount Shasta, a compound stratovolcano rising out of the sagebrush plains of Siskiyou County, is not considered a difficult climb by experienced mountaineers. But the fact that five living glaciers drape its flanks, and it generates avalanches, blizzards, and rock fall, should engender a healthy respect for its objective dangers. Gary Oye, a recreational officer for the Mount Shasta Ranger District in the town of Mount Shasta, informed us that since record keeping began in 1916, thirty-five people had died from the effects of gravity aggravated by lack of experience, poor judgment, and just plain old bad luck.

A month before this third attempt, Claire, the resident nutritionist and gourmet cook, swore we'd make the summit if we ate a proper diet.

"Fatty foods like cheese and beef jerky won't be good at those altitudes," she asserted after studying some material on high altitude physiology. "If we increase carbohydrates, snack a lot, and drink water at regular intervals, you'll see a big difference in our performance. Let's take munchies like raisins, apricots, cashews, and sesame seeds."

I was more concerned about engineering an interesting way up the mountain. If this was to be the final attempt, then it had to succeed. But I was bored with slogging up the south side "tourist route," spending the night at Helen Lake surrounded by noisy clusters of summit hopefuls. Then I found an article Steve Roper, an accomplished mountaineer, had written for *Ascent Journal* in 1968. In his photographs, the north side of Shasta looked like a different peak: remote, serene, a classic pyramid draped with glaciers and bristling with dramatic ridges. His detailed description of the broad ridge between the Hotlam and the Bolam Glaciers cinched it for me. Our pilgrimage would ascend a classic route well within our climbing abilities.

Now it was May. The weather had stabilized. We were experienced, well equipped, physically fit, and motivated. The armada of storm cells tacked northeast, just the break we needed.

"Saddle up," I said. "Let's do it!"

Sounding more confident than I felt, I let Max lead us out of the shelter of timberline into a wide, snowy corridor. He was carrying blue nylon saddlebags stuffed with Science Diet kibbles, a small medical kit, vitamins, food and water bowls, a thirty-foot lead, rubber boots, a home-sewn Gore-Tex raincoat, and, rolled into a tight blue sausage on top, his home-sewn Gore-Tex fiberfill parka with wool lining. His claws were natural crampons that would work as well as our metal ones.

The eastern boundary of our route was a tapering "Great

Wall of China" formed of basalt, a lateral moraine deposited by
the glacier. Krumholtz pine, pruned to low shrubbery by seasonal
hurricane-force winds, stood sentinel on the ramparts to the
wall. Behind us, a dark monolith rose like the prow of an oil
tanker. Through intermittent showers of cold rain, we ascended
a steepening snow slope to 11,000 feet, where the wall tapered
out. There, against a large boulder, we hacked a tent platform
into the consolidated snow, carving a kitchen complete with
benches and a cook top.

Secure in our alpine aerie, we watched a band of western
sky below the clouds fade from brass to salmon to lavender to
indigo. We wriggled into our down bags, and the Brittany curled
up in the vestibule of the tent, cozy in his insulated parka and
looking for all the world like a big blue armadillo. He smelled
like a bag of wet Fritos corn chips. As I lay there amid the measured soughing of two exhausted climbers, I sensed our margin of
success had been compressed somewhat by the unsettled weather

on one hand and the condition of those glistening slopes above us on the other. A few degrees of temperature would dictate whether we continued upward the next day or retreated once again. Even though we had crampons and ice axes, if we could not kick steps, the vertiginous terrain would become a death trap. The dark silence of the mountain enveloped our bivouac, leaving me to deal in my own way with images that floated through the penumbra of sleep, images of rock fall, altitude sickness, exhaustion, and blizzards.

As if with a flourish of cymbals and trumpets, the sun exploded over the eastern horizon revealing a near-perfect day for climbing: little wind, mild temperatures, and an infinity of blue sky. The warming rays of the sun dissipated my nocturnal apprehensions like so much valley fog. After a breakfast of oatmeal, apricots, French bread, and hot tea, I watched Claire cinch the last strap on her crampons. Then she carefully slipped a plastic film canister into her parka pocket. The ashes the canister contained represented more than a decade of unconditional love, companionship, and fond memories.

Wearing his harness, Max led us up the first pitch through steepening couloirs guarded by volcanic towers. As we gained elevation by kicking steps and jamming our ice axes into the crusty snow, the panorama behind us expanded, revealing the town of Weed, a ribbon of highway cutting across sagebrush-covered lava flows, and, floating like a mirage over the northern horizon, a snow-covered peak in Oregon.

After we had climbed steadily for a few hours, the steep snowfields just beneath the summit began to take their toll. The sky darkened to rich cobalt, and we found ourselves gasping in the thin atmosphere like catfish out of water. Our movements became mechanical: set the axe, kick a hole, step up, reset the axe, exhale, rest. Even though our stomachs were queasy and our throats felt like the Mongolian steppes, Claire's formula of water and granola at regular intervals seemed to be working. Max soldiered on, scampering up the steep snowfields and over rock outcroppings like a mountain goat. Soon we were scrambling across frozen rubble on the summit ridge, stung by sulfurous gases drifting over us from fumaroles downslope. We struggled onward, driven by little more than grim determination and Claire's admonition that "this is absolutely the last time we do this." Then, at last, there was no more mountain to climb.

We dropped our ice axes and embraced while a wave of emotion washed over us, laced with remembrances from dozens of wilderness trips together and the realization that Old Man Red finally had made it to the very top. Claire knelt on the crusted snow and gently placed the film container into a crevice in the volcanic conglomerate. Since that day, whenever the occasion arises to cruise north along Interstate Highway 5 past Dunsmuir and on toward Weed and the Oregon border beyond, we watch the white pyramid of Mount Shasta rise majestically above the sagebrush-covered horizon—and we think of Red and all the pleasure his company gave us over the years.

Max had never been on a canoe trip longer than a brief cruise along the shoreline of San Francisco Bay from the Golden Gate Bridge to Sausalito, so we decided to continue the tradition of cross training that we had begun with Red. Ninety miles north of Vancouver on the coast of British Columbia lies Desolation Sound Provincial Park—20,000 acres of fiords, estuaries, channels, straits, islands, and thickly forested coastal hills dropping straight down to the water. To the west, serving as a great barrier, Vancouver Island protects the park not only from the pulse of open ocean swells but also from the unfettered fetch of Pacific storms. On the eastern horizon, sculptured crests of granite peaks wearing tattered shawls of snow rise above the forests. Great pods of orcas cruise through the channels in search of salmon. Oysters and pastel-colored starfish encrust the rocky shores, alternately exposed, then covered by fifteen-foot tides. We decided to ignore the observation Captain Vancouver made during a visit in 1792, that the area "afforded not a single prospect that was pleasing to the eye, the smallest recreation on shore, no animal nor vegetable food, excepting a very scanty proportion."

The park seemed the ideal destination for a six-day sojourn by fiberglass ocean canoes in August 1986, with my sister Carole and her husband, Jean, whom I nicknamed the Counselor. They were both attorneys who lived in Philadelphia. To join us, they rode a westbound train over the Rockies from Toronto to

Vancouver, host to Expo 86. From Vancouver we hopped a series of ferries north to Okeover Inlet, our launching site.

Max had known something was up well before we left our house in Mill Valley. An experienced wild-country traveler by then, he had spotted the staging of tents, food, cookware (including a mountain stove and coupler), outdoor clothing, sleeping bags, and the like. By the time we arrived at our launching site and strolled into the Okeover Resort, which was managed by an affable and accommodating woman named Youtah, on the shores of Okeover Inlet, the dog had begun to vibrate like an organic tuning fork. To him this was beginning to shape up as a Brittany's dream: lots of wild country stretching out across fiords covered with a tapestry of water birds and a smorgasbord of intoxicating smells.

We ran into trouble 200 yards from the dock. The Counselor, sitting in the stern of his 18-foot fiberglass ocean-going canoe, thrashed the inlet unmercifully with his rented state-of-the-art bent shaft paddle, sending the craft first this way, then that, first to the port, then to the starboard. At that rate, the mileage to our first camp some five miles away would triple. Carole, sitting in the elevated bow, was not averse to criticizing his technique in colorful terms, thus adding lighter fluid to the proverbial fire, as it were. To quell what appeared to be an incipient mutiny before our maritime venture had even begun, I pulled alongside and administered a short canoe-paddling course to the Counselor. Although his style somewhat improved thereafter, their canoe still proceeded along a sort of repetitive parabolic pattern—like the twisting geometry of DNA.

Nevertheless, the setting sun found us at the inlet I had chosen from a map reconnaissance: a nice open shoreline of granite, sloping gently to the water and carpeted with caribou moss. A fresh-water runnel gurgled into the inlet not one hundred yards away. While unpacking our gear, I found the mountain stove and the fuel bottle, but no pump, or coupler, as the Counselor referred to it uncountable times thereafter—the essential connection between the two. I even asked Claire if she had seen it or knew where it had been packed. Without it, we could not operate the stove. A sinking feeling, like the kind that hits you when you lock yourself out of your car on the wrong side of town, compounded by the realization that we had five more days of this maritime excursion, squirmed in my solar

plexus. The Counselor picked up on this oversight right away. "You forgot the stove coupler? How could an experienced wilderness guide do that? This is going to be more of a survival experience than I thought. Raw fish and oysters for a week." Looking at Carole, he said, "And he's the only thing between us and the Russians?" He even offered to represent Claire pro bono in the divorce proceedings. As luck would have it, I found a rusted grate lying in the grass not far from camp. We would have to make do with cook fires and pray for dry weather.

The next day we paddled thirteen miles north and east into the Desolation Sound country, settling into a lovely base camp along a gentle granite shoreline backed by a sheer cliff with a thicket of pines at its base. For the next four days, Max was a blur of constant motion, power paddling across the lagoon, sprinting up and down the caribou-moss-lined shore, peering out the bow of the canoe between Claire's knees as we explored the glacier-carved fiords, islands, and inlets, racing up the trail to a fresh water lake for more power paddling, sinking into REM sleep, paws twitching almost as soon as his head hit the sleeping pad beneath the awning of our tent. Max had a distinctive swimming style. It wasn't really a dog paddle in the traditional sense. He was so powerfully built and so wild about any physical challenge that it was as if he was trying to gallop through the lake; his head and forequarters would rise up and literally create a bow wave. It was almost as much fun to watch Max swim as it was to hear the Counselor say things like "My God, look at that crescent moon sailing over the ridgeline. And that planet tagging along behind. That's gorgeous. We just don't have anything like this in Philadelphia." Too soon for my taste, the journey ended and we all returned to our respective corners of civilization.

Max's end came suddenly and unexpectedly. Even though his boisterous, push-the-envelope, live-fast-and-die-young attitude should have forewarned us, it didn't. It hit us hardest that Sunday afternoon as we were standing under a canopy of live oaks and fragrant bay laurel trees near an outcropping of lichen-covered boulders, an island of gray and green in a sea of tawny oat grass. The low October sun streaming under the branches raised a thin dew on our foreheads. I replaced my gloves and resumed digging in the rocky soil, being careful not to disturb Maxwell's lifeless form, which lay nearby. Below us the homes and streets of our neighborhood filled a shallow valley, flanked by a thirsty row of trees marching south along Salt Creek toward Richardson Bay.

We should have heeded the early signs of banditry he exhibited as a puppy when Claire regularly found her nylons, shoes, cosmetics, underwear, and a favorite running hat chewed up under the coffee table. His genius at spotting a quick opportunity to race down the street to visit a girlfriend should have been a clue. The fact that the trainer identified him early on as an alpha dog who fought Claire constantly for second ranking in the pack should have tightened our rein on him. Claire was taking the loss hard. Despite his trying personality, gradually he had become an extra layer of security for her during my absences: a walking companion, a shopping buddy. She regularly groomed his thick coat and made sure no foxtails invaded his paws.

While Claire attended evening classes, Max and I would stroll south along the trace of the Northwestern Pacific Railway, savoring fragrances of suppertime borne on the cooling air. Once we were well on the path and away from traffic, I would slip the training collar off, then watch him explode into full gallop and disappear around the bend in a cloud of dust. I trusted him to U-turn as he'd been trained to do, two hundred yards from East Blithedale, and rocket past me, faking this way and that to avoid a playful tap on the backside. The night he disappeared, platinum light from a bloated harvest moon washed the meadows; the chilled air was laced with deer musk. He made his U-turn, raced past me, and disappeared up the path toward home. That was the last time I saw him alive.

Four agonizing days passed with no sign of Max, no word of his whereabouts. The posters we had distributed in the community and tacked up on telephone poles all the way to Corte Madera had elicited no response. On Sunday afternoon while Claire was off shopping, the cordless phone I had stashed nearby while working in the organic garden rang. I answered it. It was a woman riding her bicycle along East Blithedale; she had discovered Max lying in a shallow ditch across from Cala Foods and had taken the time to call the number stamped on his collar:

a rare act of kindness in a hurried world. I thanked her, hung up, and raced to the truck, thinking I could retrieve his body before Claire returned. As luck would have it, she caught me halfway down Underhill Road, driving in the opposite direction. From the expression on my face through the open window, she could tell the news was not good. I told her I would handle it, but she would have none of it. She parked her Volvo and jumped in the passenger side of the truck. "He wasn't the easiest dog to live with," she said with a quavering voice. "But I just can't let you do this alone."

When we located him in the ditch he was stretched out in the weeds, muzzle cradled between his paws, stone dead—looking for all the world as if he'd merely fallen asleep in an unlikely place. Claire even felt his side for breathing. We gathered him up in a paint-stained drop cloth I had brought along, then hoisted him into the truck for one last ride through the neighborhood: a strange journey without his ecstatic face in the side-view mirror—lips peeling back, inhaling a smorgasbord of odors suffused on the slipstream.

I carried him from the truck up the steep meadow trail that he so loved as a gateway to adventure beyond, whether it be an ordinary after-work walk in the hills or a run along Blithedale Ridge. The most difficult part turned out to be moving Max's rigid body, shrouded in the drop cloth, to the grave. It was if we were crossing a psychic Rubicon with no chance of redemption for our challenging relationship with this dog. We laid him down gently, brushing the twigs and leaves from his muzzle, then carefully backfilling the depression with loose soil and rocks. The heavy labor over at last, a stillness—heartbreaking and final—suffused the hazy afternoon. I took off my gloves and looked over at Claire and said, "Well, I guess that's . . ." and then broke down in tears. Four days of anxiety and foreboding welled up in both of us simultaneously. We embraced desperately, as if to reassure each other that his death had been merely a predictable consequence of his banditry. At that moment on the hill, we realized he finally had gotten away with the most valuable of possessions—our hearts. And in so doing had torn a gaping hole in the fabric of our lives.

Try as we might to rationalize his untimely end at the age of four, our thoughts kept looping back to our husbandry of this difficult dog. Thankfully, Claire never even hinted at blaming me for the loss. I was harder on myself, and still am to this day. From the time he disappeared, we vowed never again to allow a Brittany to romp about unfettered unless he was hunting. To hammer our fragile psyches even further, dreams about him followed his death like ephemeral echoes of his short but boisterous life.

> Claire and I are in the garage looking for some household item. Suddenly Max appears in full color, prancing back and forth across the cement floor the way he used to when he wanted to go for a run or a walk through the neighborhood. I approach him to discover that

his double coat is full and soft, his bony frame
solid to the touch, his nose cold and moist. I
say to Claire, "Hey! Do you know he's real? It's
really Max!"

From my bed, I hear the scratch of nails
spinning frantically across the oak parquet floor
of the second floor entryway, then the thump,
thump, thump of Max bounding down the
stairs, followed by the impact of his ecstatic
body on our bed. I wake to the drumming of
rain in the downspout.

Even our neighbor Joe told us he dreamt about Max running
into his garage smeared with mud from the playground near
Edna McGuire Elementary School, and hitting him square in
the crotch of his crisp khaki trousers with both front paws.

A week after Max's death, while making breakfast,
Claire's bitterness and disappointment welled up once again.

"It'll be a cold day in hell before I have anything more to
do with the Catholic Church," she said. "Every day he was missing I said twelve Rosaries and as many Hail Marys. For thirteen
years in this neighborhood we've seen neglected dogs running
around loose, no leashes, and nothing ever happens to them. Max
couldn't travel unescorted fifteen feet from the kitchen door to
the backyard gate. My friends tell me Max had a better life than
most kids. Why are we being punished? At least we'll always
know where he is now, small comfort that is."

She began to cry again softly—like the misty rain that
drifts over Blithedale Ridge on an overcast day—without missing

one step in the pork tureen recipe and the spicy chicken nuggets she was preparing for a birthday party the following night or the stew she was cooking for our supper. She checked the roma tomatoes she was drying in the dehydrator, then tossed a load of clothes into the washing machine. Her thin frame looked even bonier that night.

"Have you lost weight?" I asked.

"About a pound since last Wednesday night."

It was Sunday; at that rate, she would disappear entirely by February 15. Next morning she whipped up a sour cream-pecan coffeecake for my office and made breakfast. On the way to the car, she paused at the railing of the entry deck and gazed up at the meadow that was just beginning to glow through morning fog. The cluster of rocks and live oaks that is Max's final resting place floated gauzy and gray-green in a sea of tawny oat grass. She wiped her eyes, then wiped the dew off the windshield of our aging Volvo, and drove me to the bus. Then she returned home to get ready for work at the architecture office in Sausalito.

Max's exuberant persona had such a hold on us that sometimes it was difficult to discriminate between deep dreaming and waking fantasy. Not long after he died, I jotted these notes in my journal:

> By the time I hit the end of the street and start
> up the trail into open space, I'm glad I wore
> tights, a polypro shirt, windbreaker, knit cap,
> and gloves. The November air is cold. The
> steep trail, flanked by a ravine, slices straight up

through the beaten down oat straw that was so dangerous to Max's feet and nose in late May and early June. The vicious dart-shaped foxtail seeds with backward pointing bristles rode his thick ivory-and-cinnamon coat and burrowed their way in between his toes, guaranteeing a big vet bill if we didn't pluck them out after every run.

Blowing like a draft horse, I pass a cluster of gray rocks the size of a small house nested in a tight grove of oak and bay laurel trees. On the downhill side of this complex, Max lies under adobe clay and shards of rock, tucked into the massive root system of a coast live oak and camouflaged by a quilt of prickly oak leaves. His untimely death a month ago tugs at me, breaks my stride, triggers a visceral longing for his exuberant company on these runs through the leonine hills of Marin County. The sun has dropped behind Blithedale Ridge, and darkness is growing in the trees. Beyond the ridge, patterns of praying hands or crowns of thorns in the overarching oak and laurel limbs are silhouetted against the salmon-colored sky. Across the bay, orange sunlight flashing off the Bank of America building transforms it into an urban lighthouse.

I move on up the slope toward Camino Alto, feeling warmth flow at last into my thigh and calf muscles. Downhill out of the corner of my eye, I sense more than see a flicker of movement, an ivory-cinnamon presence streaking from the direction of the rocks and driving powerfully uphill through the dun-colored grass. I can almost hear excited keening: that familiar urge to run full out, ecstatic huffing. Suddenly I'm infused with a sense of energy, a powerful desire to see around the next bend, beyond the next ridgeline, a compulsion to move unfettered across open ground.

Down the road, around the bend, then through the gate onto the fire road, we're running flat out, feet hardly hitting the asphalt. After tunneling through the long tree-covered corridor leading up the fire trail to the top of the ridge, we break out into the open, blinking against the bright neon sky; turn right; and follow a series of looping contours along the north side of Blithedale Ridge. The chilled air is fragrant with bay laurel and chinquapin and decaying redwood needles.

Soon we're doubling back along the spine of the ridge, where the bare bones of the Franciscan formation poke through adobe clay. To the west, Mount Tamalpais looms in the gloaming, a huge pyramid black against the dimming sky. Here and there I crunch through frozen puddles of rainwater, shattering ice like thin panes of glass. We drive strongly up the last rocky pitch, then begin looping down the trail, descending into pockets of moist darkness, rising once again on the spine of the ridge into brighter air. To the north, the lights of Corte Madera float in the dusk like some galactic mother ship.

I miss Max's addiction to adventure in open country, his superb physical condition, his brawny approach to life. When he was only a few months old I took him to Rodeo Beach and threw a tennis ball into the surf for him. Even though he had only seen the ocean twice before, he leaped without hesitation into the churning water, plowed through the waves, grabbed the ball, and bodysurfed the crashing breakers back to the beach. The fifty-degree water didn't even faze him.

The fire road just above Camino Alto is so dark I can't see any definition in the path, so we throttle back to a sensible pace until we hit smooth asphalt on the road. I sense a surge of power and speed and excitement beside me during the customary sprint up to the crest of the hill. Cooling down as the narrow path descends, I admire the pulsing lights of the City silhouetting the cluster of rocks and bay laurels that is Max's home. Then he is gone, and I am alone with the luminous horizon and the chill of the night air.

Blazer

Five weeks after Max's death in October 1988, I drove our truck down the coast to the little village of Montara. It was a Saturday, and as far as Claire knew, I was attending a continuing education class in Sunnyvale. I really did, but unbeknownst to her, the class had let out early and I had slipped over to the coast to inspect a litter of Brittanys I'd heard about.

Just before dusk, Marilyn Maxwell, a well-known breeder of high-quality Brittanys, led me from her modest ranch house to the backyard, where she kept spotless kennels constructed of cyclone fencing and concrete slabs. Comfortable plywood houses protected the dogs from fog that drifted in reefs across the coastline and from winter storms that raced in from the Pacific Ocean. Marilyn introduced me to a five-month-old pup with markings that were startlingly similar to Max's: the same clove-shaped white stripe bisecting his face, the same prominent occipital bump, the same ivory-and-cinnabar coat. But something

"Marilyn told me she bred this litter toward a show coat. But he should have good hunting qualities too," I explained.

Regardless of all the fondling and petting, the pup remained frozen in a standing position, as if he expected to be slaughtered and eaten at any second.

His official AKC registered name, Maxwell's Lost River Trailblazer, soon shrank to Blazer or the even more diminutive Blaze. Eventually, he wove himself into our lives and our daily schedules. He moved into Max's old syrup barrel in the backyard and took up the position of sentry and wildlife observer. Cautious and submissive, he was pretty much Max's opposite in temperament. But he reserved the right to bust out of his reticent personality once in a while just to remind us that above all he was—a Brittany.

One evening in the spring, just as dusk erased the contours of our organic garden, Claire appeared with a flashlight. Proudly I showed her the fruits, so to speak, of three hours of labor: two dozen bare root Tioga strawberry plants tucked into the double-dug soil that I had enriched with blood meal, bone meal, and compost. A green two-foot-high fence surrounded the bed as protection from Blazer.

"That uphill side looks loose," she admonished. "He could sneak under." He is her dog; she knew his devious, scheming mind best.

"Nah. Look at those rocks. No way can he get under there."

Two days later, while surveying what looked like an artillery range—tender strawberry plants scattered, buried, and chomped, with craters everywhere—I fantasized how his hide would look tanned and hung on the den wall: art deco Brittany.

As an amateur organic gardener, I have average patience; I'm willing to wait two years before harvesting asparagus spears. I can resist the temptation to let new strawberry blossoms form fruit the first year. But these Brittanys we've owned over twenty years have stretched that patience close to the snapping point on more than one occasion. The Mystery of the Missing Asparagus is a perfect example. One year we awaited the best crop of asparagus ever from mature crowns invigorated by sweet spring rains. I even launched an early attack on marauding beetles. Nothing. The neighbors were disappointed. It was a mystery until one evening I saw Blazer holding down the protective wire mesh with his front paws while maneuvering his muzzle through the opening to nip off the new spears at ground level, neat as a scythe. When I confronted him about it, he laid the big browns on me as if to ask, "Hey. Where's the hollandaise sauce?"

When I think back to the hours I have spent torturing my back muscles to dog-proof the garden (railroad ties under the gates, extra cyclone fencing across the side yard, fencing around all the planted areas), I sometimes question my sanity. But the question at hand was: can dogs and gardens coexist? After all this time, I realize I had done things backwards. I should have enclosed the Brittanys instead of the garden. Breeders build runs

of cyclone fencing with comfortable kennels at one end. The key is starting the pups young, so they don't know anything better.

I'm convinced the best solution for the gardening dog owner is to confine planted areas to raised beds and restrict the dog to his run when no one is supervising him. Freedom happens when master is puttering around the flowerbed or double-digging the main garden for a new garlic crop. It is too late for us; we've opted for canine freedom over human sanity. Our garden may look like San Quentin, but at least the summer squashes don't have that lingering ammonia flavor. Any serious gardeners who also happen to own a Brittany should do themselves a favor—fence him in.

The first inkling that we had acquired a schemer sent chills up my spine. At first I thought a genetic thread to the infamous bandit Max had survived in this generation of dogs. One morning, I was in the basement building a potting bench for our organic garden. Blazer, who had been with us just a few months now, was comfortably ensconced in the condo I had built for Red some years before.

So there I was using a skill saw on 2 x 6s, when suddenly I was eyeball to eyeball with a seven-month-old pup peering up between my legs; not good, should the spinning carbide-tipped saw blade come in contact with pink puppy flesh. I gathered the pup in my arms and carried him to the enclosure door, gently placing him inside the 12 x 12-foot space where he had access to water, a new insulated fiberglass kennel, and a hatch to the backyard. I carefully closed the door and dropped the galvanized gate latch into its cradle. The string I had tied to the lever on the latch in case I inadvertently locked myself in hung down about a foot inside the enclosure.

I went back to work, firing up the circular saw, which ripped through redwood beams as if they were made of papier-mâché. I glanced down and there he was again, staring up between my legs with huge chestnut eyes. "What are you doing, Papa?" he seemed to be saying. I felt a moment of anxiety; either the late shifts at the FBI office had scrambled my medulla oblongata or my engineering was defective. I repeated the routine once again: pick up the pup, open the door, place him in the enclosure, close the door, drop the latch positively, affirm in my own mind that it was secure. Then I fired up the saw and continued my work. The third time I saw the big browns peering up at me through a cloud of sawdust, I damn near freaked out. This was getting spooky. It was as if we had acquired a poltergeist capable of drifting right through physical barriers such as 2 x 4 walls and locked doors.

This time I picked up the pup and followed the previous routine with one variation; afterwards I walked over to the main basement door opposite the enclosure, opened it, and stepped outside. I looked back through the crack in the door hoping to verify that I wasn't losing my mind after all. I didn't have long to wait. Thirty seconds after I had closed the door, I watched Blazer rise up on his hind legs and lunge at the safety string with his teeth. The first time he missed. On the second try he caught it dead center and pulled it sharply down while simultaneously punching the door with his paws. The door flew open, and he danced through and started looking around for me. End of mystery.

Before he was a year old, we experienced another mystery. The toilet paper roll in the upstairs guest bathroom kept getting shredded despite the door being closed most of the time. It looked as if someone had shot it at close range with number eight birdshot or used it for a piñata. We became even more careful about closing the door. This went on for weeks until one morning we heard the doorknob click. I raced upstairs and caught the pup just before he shredded another roll. Apparently he had refined the technique he'd learned in the basement so that he now could twist the knob with his paws and push the door open. Lacing the roll with hot sauce was out, and we were fresh out of ideas. So we just had to let him grow out of that destructive habit.

There were other mysterious occurrences. One Christmas Eve we found a terrific deal on a twelve-foot-high Noble fir from the deep Oregon woods. We made a fresh cut at the base, fastened it in the metal stand, then poured a steaming pint of Claire's special elixir—water, corn syrup, bleach, a few drops of liquid iron—into the reservoir. Adorned with sparkly lights and an array of vintage ornaments, it looked handsome indeed. What mystified us was why the reservoir kept drying out—until Claire noticed a whiff of fir sap on Blazer's breath.

The Brittany cross-training program continued with lessons in organized foot racing. One year I convinced Claire and Blazer to enter the annual Federal Law Enforcement Officers' foot race, known as the Supersleuth, through the Presidio of San Francisco. Actually, I didn't have to convince Blazer. "Run" is one of those words you spelled around him, along with "walk," "cookie," "dinner," and "hunting." Accepting the fact that guests were not eligible for awards, Claire agreed to run at a leisurely pace, "Just a fun run, you understand, not to compete with anybody." She fitted Blazer with an unofficial red-and-white running bib marked "Snoopysleuth 1994 Number 14," and stepped up to the starting line.

After an abortive start punctuated by Blazer's excited howling and the blast from a .357 Magnum (someone had forgotten the starter gun), they were off. At the one-mile marker, where the eight-kilometer route splits from the two-mile run, Claire heard heavy footfalls behind her, labored breathing, and vocal self-flagellation. "Oh God. I went the wrong way. I wanted to do the two-mile fun run. Now I'm on the eight kilometer. I'm going to die!" Morie Greenspan, a large U.S. postal inspector, had screwed up big time. Now he was being swept by a mob of over-exercised and underfed sleuths straight toward anaerobic doom. Delivering a pep talk worthy of Bill Walsh when the Forty Niners are losing, Claire took Morie in tow and coaxed him down the hill, under Park Presidio Avenue, past Mountain Lake, and up the gut-wrenching, sun-blasted eternity of the golf course hill.

Pausing twice to allow Blazer to unload, Claire and Morie dashed across the finish line covered with sweat. It wasn't until the official results had been announced that Claire realized she had placed first among women in her age category (forty something) and second among all female runners. God bless you, Morie Greenspan, wherever you are.

Claire's tendency to include Blazer in her comings and goings sometimes led to comic situations. Early one morning in May, she and Blazer drove the old Toyota truck a mile and a half down the road for its spring tune-up. At the repair shop, she hooked Blazer to a rope for the walk back home (she'd forgotten his leash). Hoisting the carry strap of her rolled up Jazzercise mat—the one she'd need for that evening's class—over her shoulder, she stepped on down the road, wearing an oversized sweatshirt, beat up running shoes, and jeans ripped at the knee; her hair was not yet coifed, and her "face" had not yet been applied. At the East Blithedale crosswalk she paused for the signal. A homeless man pushing a Safeway cart along the opposite sidewalk glanced over and gave her a big smile and an exuberant double thumbs up. Right on, sister! Homeless solidarity.

Brittanys sometimes save you money. One afternoon Claire and a friend pulled up at the Golden Gate Bridge tollbooth, southbound, to meet me for dinner in San Francisco. Unless you had three people in the car, the toll was three dollars. Blazer was sitting in the back seat wearing, for some reason, a San Francisco Giants baseball cap. As Claire held her three dollars out the window, the toll collector waved her on through. They were twenty-five yards down the road before the collector yelled, "Hey wait a minute! That's a dog." Too late: a three-dollar freebie.

Max had been a Don Juan with the neighborhood ladies, but I'm convinced Blazer attracted some love interest with his shy, retiring, and vulnerable demeanor. One Saturday afternoon he reacted as any red-blooded guy would if, say, Heather Locklear paraded provocatively by the kitchen door without a stitch on—lust-crazed pandemonium. While he tried to dismantle the kitchen slider to get at Hanna, the Welsh springer spaniel who was wiggling seductively outside, Claire yelled down to me in the backyard for help. Unaware that Hanna was in heat, I hoisted Blazer into the back of the truck with her for the ride back to her house up on the hill. Halfway out of the garage, the truck began rocking like a cement mixer. I raced around to the back, disengaged the gyrating canines, and pulled Blazer out to ride in the cab. Hanna took that opportunity to leap over the tailgate into my arms. Somehow I hoisted her back into the truck while Blazer, newly aroused, attacked my right leg, causing both of us to collapse on the driveway. With the crazed Brittany locked on to my leg and humping like a jackhammer, I struggled to my feet and finally gained the upper hand. Only then did I notice the hysterical laughter of Joe and Barbara across the street. "Should we call 911?" they shouted, "or do you have things under control?"

After I presented Blazer to Claire that rainy night in 1988, our initial apprehensions about skipping the puppy phase evaporated when we realized he was the opposite of Max's headstrong, boisterous, Alpha dog, live-fast-and-die-young persona. Our first outing after his arrival was an evening walk along the trace of the Northwestern Pacific Railway to familiarize him with his surroundings. An autumn storm had left cool dry air in its wake, and a frisky breeze slapped overhead branches into wild gesticulations. More than once, Blazer dived between my feet, whimpering in fright at some imagined terror. I knew then that our husbandry of this dog would be vastly different from our warden-like experience with Max. Blazer turned out to be responsive and obedient, with a more affectionate approach to humans.

You couldn't ask for a better canine trail companion. But his initiation to wilderness travel at an early age triggered some interesting reactions. On the second day of a cross-country traverse of the Crystal Range in Desolation Wilderness just west of Lake Tahoe, we settled into a camp at 9,000 feet near a jewel-like tarn upholstered with fine meadow grass. A copse of feathery hemlock trees encircled by willow brush was the centerpiece. As Claire and I staked out the tent and fluffed up our sleeping bags, we noticed the Brittany scuffling around in hemlock and willow branches at the edge of the meadow. We watched him circle and circle, as some dogs will do before they lie down (perhaps a vestige of their genetic linkage to wolves who typically scour out a nest in the snow with such antics). He chewed off protruding branches and circled some more until he had his bivouac just right. Then he lay down and tucked into a tight doughnut, looking for all the world like a big chipmunk asleep in his nest. Being a backpacking neophyte, he had no clue he was supposed to sleep with us at night. When we moved him over to the tent, we saw what might have triggered all this wild behavior—a swatch of coyote undercoat snagged on a nearby hemlock branch.

On these backcountry trips coyotes have always been a seldom-seen, almost phantom-like presence. While cross-country skiing in the Upper Truckee Valley one gorgeous spring day, we watched a lone coyote traverse the snowy flanks of Red Lake Peak at almost 10,000 feet. What it hoped to find up there baffled us, unless it was the sheer exuberance of cruising the ridges in such stunningly beautiful weather. The soprano keening of coyotes never fails to send a thrill down my spine as I listen from within a flickering cone of campfire light either alone or with a companion. But wily coyote may be pushing his luck. Not satisfied with the natural menu of mice, rats, ground squirrels, gophers, rabbits, insects, reptiles of all types, amphibians, fruits, and birds, they've developed a taste for lamb and calf steaks. Recently, coyotes have begun to test the wildland-urban interface by making off with Fido's kibble and, more frequently it seems, Fido himself, along with the family cat for dessert. In southern Marin County, we hear them at night on a ridge near our home, where they've established a territory and appear to be raising families—five to seven pups born in the spring. At dusk one evening we saw a big male sashaying past our garden gate on Underhill Road, swinging his bushy tail, bold as hell.

Although Blazer has escaped run-ins with coyotes, I still break out in a cold sweat when I remember that he nearly fell victim to a miscalculation in tilted terrain of the Emigrant Wilderness near Sonora Pass several years ago. Claire and I were on a three-day cross-country traverse of 10,000-foot Granite Dome when we encountered some tricky ground—a short wall flanking a gap through which our route would descend to remote and lovely Iceland Lake. Halfway up the wall, I climbed across a fissure in the granite that must have been almost a foot wide at the top, tapering down into darkness. Right behind me, Blazer lunged upward, spun out, and fell into the crack, wedged by his pack. Then I realized my mistake in not removing his wet and slippery leather Australian sheepdog boots before we began the climb. Had he not been wearing his pack, he probably would have dropped into the crack out of reach and become inextricably wedged. Given the intensity of Claire's feelings for Blazer, I would now be calling a bachelor pad home if I had not been able to extricate him.

When the workday routine gets to you, sometimes you have to break away. Blazer and I spotted a window of opportunity in April 1997, when Claire would be traveling to Carmel with her sister Linda to help their mother celebrate her eightieth birthday. An epic Sierra Nevada snow pack was evaporating fast under the spring sun, so we would have to move quickly. I loaded the old Toyota truck with skis, food, camping gear, and an excited Brittany, and rattled on up to the high country. We found a suitable trailhead along Highway 89 south of Lake Tahoe and soon were climbing on skins (and paws) over ideal corn snow through a mixed lodgepole pine-Shasta red fir forest. Late in the afternoon, we dug in a snug bivouac at 9,000 feet on the side of a ridge right at timberline.

After supper, the nine-year-old Brittany—tucked into his

homemade parka—soaked up the radiant heat of a campfire, oblivious to the nighttime spectacle unfolding overhead: Mars glowing orange in the southeastern quadrant of the sky, the comet Hale-Bopp floating like a phosphorescent feather over the western horizon. Blazer's quiet company was the perfect complement to these solo ventures. Tucked into the mountain tent in his Gore-Tex parka, wearing the wool socks Claire had insisted I throw in the pack, he drifted off almost instantly into a whimpering and running dreamland.

The next morning, under a deep ultramarine sky brushed with milky cirrus, we two middle-aged mountaineers launched from the ridge and sailed 2,000 feet down the mountain. While I carved telemarks across the softening meadows, Blazer raced alongside in a state of canine ecstasy, inhaling the alpine fragrances—reverting to puppydom for a brief interlude of unfettered romping.

As addicted as we both were to wild country, Blazer and I took every opportunity to explore it. Late one summer I tried to interest the usual suspects in a backpacking trip to Northern California. No takers. Claire had social commitments. I had burned out my younger brother years before on some rigorous Sierra forays. But there was one guy I could always count on for an enthusiastic response. It didn't take me long to load the truck with food and equipment. Before long Blazer and I were well along the interminable Interstate 5 corridor headed toward Redding and beyond. My trip journal picks up the story from there.

Even at eleven years old, Blazer pulls on the twenty-foot retractable lead as if he's a damned Malamute in the Iditarod. He's hauling me up a trail that slices through a forest of Shasta red fir and Douglas fir parallel to Canyon Creek. Then the path forks. We bear to the left and climb over a broad ridge to the Red Rock Creek drainage. I feel as if I'm behind a ski boat, hanging on for dear life. The trail is a blur, as are panoptic vistas that appear from time to time through openings in the forest. If I glanced over at them, I'd go ass over teakettle off the trail and down the slope into the manzanita, pack and all. It feels as if we're doing about four miles per hour, but later calculations put our trail speed at a little over two miles per hour. The Old Guy actually canters up some slopes.

Despite Blazer's age, it takes some concentration for me to manage him. Only another dog could explain why he insists on peeing off his right side with his head pointing downhill. To accomplish that when we're headed uphill, he must reverse course, walk downhill, pee on his right side, then pirouette to his left, wrapping the leash around the bedding sausage on top of his pack. My thirty-five-pound pack makes bending over to unwind the mess a chore. Why can't he just pee every seventy-five yards on the right side going uphill? The mysteries of the Brittany mind. Then he dunks himself and his pack in every stream that cuts the trail. Although balanced when both are dry, the saddlebags list to starboard when wet, forcing me to shift a package of kibble or something to balance things out.

At mid morning, we're two miles from the Lover's Camp Trailhead at the beginning of a three-day sojourn to the Marble Mountain Wilderness in northern California. The road from Fort Jones to the trailhead rambled across patchwork quilts of emerald-colored alfalfa fields and neat cattle ranches of Scott Valley set against dark ridges that faded to blue in the distance. Our route will loop some twenty-miles through the northeastern portion of this wilderness: a sampling that should afford views of the limestone geology that makes this corner of the Cascade Mountains unique. I hope to see park-like subalpine meadows ringed by Shasta red fir and noble fir; Marble Mountain lying on the western horizon like some Mesozoic leviathan with its limestone bones bleaching in the stinging alpine sun; shallow lakes that invite a late afternoon swim; a fleeting glimpse, perhaps, of Sasquatch. As we gain elevation, the red fir forest opens up to a series of meadows bordered by aspens and poplars. The breeze flowing across them carries a rich fragrance of anise mixed with tarweed, laced from time to time with the acrid stench of fresh cow patties. The flower show is complex: a tapestry of sky-blue daisy-like flowers, shooting stars, Indian paintbrush, bright white sprays, purple flowers, yellow daisy-like flowers. The quaking aspens will be luminous in the fall, their leaves spinning in the wind like gold coins.

Five miles of steady uphill brings us to the crest of the main east-west ridge and the intersection with the celebrated Pacific Crest Trail. A left turn takes us east along the southern flank of the ridge. After chugging along the undulating trail for several miles, the unseasonably warm and humid weather compounded by the unobstructed rays of the sun angling in from the southwest begin to take their toll. Late summer in these mountains is supposed to be crisp and dry. This isn't crisp and dry; it feels like Belize. I keep the Brittany well watered, since he persists in pulling me up and down even the steepest sections of trail. After two more miles of uncomfortably hot humping, we leave the main trail and bushwhack though a thick stand of lodgepole pine, contouring carefully along the side of a broad ridge, using the compass and altimeter to keep us found. A third of a mile along the azimuth brings us to Gem and Jewel Lakes—little more than potholes perched on a level bench where the ridge abuts a fractured escarpment of rust-colored granite.

Our search for a decent campsite forces us across a slope covered with Manzanita brush and boulders. More than once, Blazer ends up suspended by his pack in the springy branches, dog-paddling thin air. I rescue him by his harness straps and set him down on terra firma, amazed at his determination to plow through the stuff without a whimper of complaint.

The biggest of the five lakes is flanked by a nice meadow that separates it from the last pond where salamanders sinuate along the caramel-colored bottoms of the ponds near drowned tree trunks, kicking up puffs of silt with their tails. The cliff above us glows ochre and rust in the rays of the westering sun. It is deeply fractured, with a ravine cleaving it all the way to the top. These meadows, tiny though they are, are tightly woven—like golf course putting greens. A gin-clear rivulet draining the high ridge warbles a tune to itself as it meanders through the meadow: a much more appetizing water source than the salamander aquarium we passed. My altimeter reads 6,800 feet. The country drops off abruptly to the east, affording a nice view in that direction. This will be our home for the next twenty hours.

We stretch out on the plush meadow grass while the sweat evaporates and the sun shoots orange rays at a low angle between the tree trunks. It is tempting to drift off to the sound of trickling water, but there is work to be done before sunset. Soon the mountain stove is putt-putting along with a frenetic pulse, heating the water we will need for soup and the main dish—pasta with peas and onions. Two gallons of water scooped from the rivulet hang in a bag from the nearest lodgepole pine. Like a cater-pillar cocoon, the Moss tent stands ready for our weary bodies. Lying on the grass in the Fiberfill Gore-Tex parka that Claire stitched together with her old sewing machine some years ago, Blazer resembles a gourmet Thai wrap. As I watch his paws begin to twitch, and reflect on his spirited performance today, I know that Claire is right when she says he is the best Brittany of the three we've owned over thirty years. When I bought him from Marilyn Maxwell, she assured me his lineage contained excellent show and field performers. She was right on both counts. Unlike the rough double coat of his cousin Max, Blazer's fur is like fine silk: at thirty-six pounds, he is the ideal size. The only thing missing from his genetic blue-print is a suitcase handle midway along his spine to make car travel more convenient. You can't have everything.

Now it is 7:30 p.m. in the Marble Mountain Wilderness, and my thermometer tells me it is sixty degrees—still uncomfortably warm. Bedecked with jewels, Jupiter floats incandescent in the eastern sky. The one-eighth waxing moon casts a soft pearly light across our campsite, illuminating the trunk of a huge Western white pine growing out of a boulder complex on the far side of the meadow. The feel of this saucer-shaped green tucked into the side of the ridge is isolation of the benevolent variety—privacy without a feeling of vulnera-bility: quite the opposite, actually. A site closer to the Pacific Crest Trail would generate anxieties about casual drop-ins—types who plod along the main drag, heads down, then crash on the shoulder at the end of the day without any effort to conceal their camp.

The Brittany and I settle into the small tent, him in his parka and me in my summer sleeping bag, back-to-back against whatever bumps the night might produce. By now he smells like a bran muffin gone bad, or a bag of wet Fritos Corn Chips. Although generally he's a pretty sound sleeper, inevitably he will dig his claws into my back or whimper his way through a particularly vivid dream; but I won't mind because the nine hours of snoozing slowly will erase the sleep deficit we incur at home. I will tuck scary thoughts about wilderness mishaps—like the backpacker they found stone dead in his sleeping bag, his skull crunched like a ripe melon by a black bear, or an encounter with the enigmatic Sasquatch— into the shadow of sleep. The velvet mallet descends on both our heads, and the night passes seamlessly, uneventfully, punctuated only twice by the usual heart-thumpers: a pinecone grenade dropped by a squirrel, an anonymous rustling in the brush by the lake.

At 7:00 a.m. the thermometer reads forty-six degrees. I sweated out of my summer sleeping bag several times during the night, even though I had shifted most of the down to the other side in anticipation of the warmer temperatures. The silence here is profound, broken only by a small orange helicopter clattering overhead yesterday, and today a gigantic yellow Sikorsky cargo chopper with a fuselage that looks like a rectangular piece fell out of it: probably part of a logging operation. As the sun warms the meadow, flies buzz, a few mosquitoes hum, and the grasshoppers ricochet around, making a clackity racket. Once in a while an alarmingly large bumblebee cruises by, generating a hum that sounds like human voices. My ears pricked up several times before I realized what it was.

Over a breakfast of tea, dried fruit, granola, and Neutro Lamb and Rice kibble, we scan the area with a new perspective afforded by the brightening eastern sky. The first order of business is an exploratory side trip to some lakes that look intriguing on the map. It takes us forty-five minutes to drop down the trail to Summit Lake and Summit Meadow Lake, both of which lie at the base of a seven-hundred-foot-high gray cliff. At Summit Meadow Lake, I find the skinny-dipping is about as good as you can expect this side of Cancun; you tiptoe across pieces of bark and grassy hummocks to avoid the black muck, then step into the lake, only to sink six inches into organic silt. The drowned skeletons of red firs are greasy with algae. This lake is only about four feet deep, a fact I discover after flailing out to the center, stopping, and realizing I can stand up on the squishy bottom. The lake is refreshing, not uncomfortably cold, laced as it is with horizontal bands of warmer water. It is slowly becoming a meadow through eutrophication.

At my urging, Blazer paddles out twenty yards but soon becomes alarmed at being so far from solid ground and paddles back to shore, shaking himself vigorously after hauling himself up onto the grassy bank. At first, Claire and I thought his aversion to water was a puppy thing, but he never grew out of it. Unlike Max, the power paddler, Blazer has to be coaxed into water over his head unless he's overheated. Now we lie in the fragrant meadow grass and heather, watching the sunlight slant down through red firs to ignite the lime-green surface of the lake. The sun is warm and soon we are dry, the Brittany sporting Rastafarian curls along his flanks and ears.

It would be delightful to lounge here and watch shadows lengthen, but duty calls; our next camp is seven miles away. We climb back up the switchbacks and then thread our way through the thick timber to base camp. After a light lunch, we pack up, leaving our presence in the delicate meadow undetectable—even down to the tiniest piece of tinfoil and floss. As I anticipated from the trip in, yesterday, the first three miles of the Pacific Crest Trail are rocky and hot. Epic views of distant ridges receding in shades of blue to the south, the deep gash cut by Wooley Creek on its westward plunge to the Salmon River, lure the eye to the horizon, compensating somewhat for our discomfort. We're moving west along the south flank of an east-west ridge through intermittent old growth of Shasta red fir and beautiful rust and beige meadows bedecked with flowers of every size and color. A light southerly breeze helps alleviate the natural heat we generate on the move, compounded by the ambient temperature of the air.

At the junction with the Sky High Lake Trail, Blazer's thermostat goes off the chart. He throws himself into some low fir branches and pants like a steam engine, tongue hanging out like a crimson dishrag. It is hanging down so far, I wouldn't be surprised to see it fall out of his mouth onto the dirt. I give him a quarter bottle of water and pour the rest on his head. For some reason my feet feel uncomfortable today, especially the right big and little toes— as if a tiny gnome has hopped into my boot and is sanding away with an emery board. The pad of my left foot feels like Wolfgang Puck has pounded it with one of those toothed hardwood mallets he uses for tenderizing steaks. Fully recovered by now, Blazer yanks me unmercifully down the steep trail for a mile to Frying Pan Lake. He's pulling about ten to fifteen pounds on the downhill vector, making my ankles, knees, hips, and feet feel as if I have that much more weight in my pack. Then there's the breaking action necessary to keep him from pulling me off balance. Maybe that has something to do with the condition of my feet. By the time we set our camp on a broad, rocky moraine between Lower Sky High Lake and Frying Pan Lake, it is 5:00 p.m., and we're both wasted. Upper Sky High Lake is a saucer-shaped tarn at the base of a steep ridge. The shoreline is covered with thick willow brush that obviates any campsites. A raft of mallards drifts along the far shore. Lower Sky High Lake is set in a bowl to the east of us, with no view. I like it better here on this lonely dry ridge where I can see Black Marble Mountain dominating the western horizon, and Canyon Creek Valley dropping away to the north. Meadow grass, lupine, and a dry plant that has turned a rust color with the season cover the volcanic soil. This country has the feel of Oregon about it—the spiky noble firs evoking a sense of the north woods. Where the ridges and peaks break through the mantle of forest or ground cover, you see the bare bones of dark basalt, granite, or marble. The marble formations are the most intriguing.

While mushroom soup simmers on the mountain stove, I watch alpenglow cast pastel hues on the flanks of 7,500-foot Black Marble Mountain, the centerpiece of this unusual wilderness. The guidebook tells me I am looking at a piece of the ocean floor—compressed sediments that rose up nearly four hundred million years ago, along with granitic plutons, to form the Marbles, the Siskiyous, and the Trinities to the south. A rising ocean surrounded the uplifted country, turning it into a huge island. After the waters receded, glaciers bulldozed, ground, and polished the peaks and valleys to their present shapes.

The weather has remained boringly stable, hostage to the autumn high-pressure bubble that develops over the northwest this time of year. I wouldn't mind an old-fashioned storm with menacing thunderheads bearing down on us, pregnant with rain, grumbling and growling, charged with electrons and hunting for a promontory to tempt the sky fire of Zeus. Some hail would be nice, timed of course to avoid mealtime.

The act of unplugging from the workday routine (up at 5:20 in the morning, shower, shave, eat breakfast, drive to the bus, ride to San Francisco, walk three blocks to the office, check out the Dow and NASDAQ on the Charles Schwab stock exchange marquis, arrive at the office at 7:40 a.m., leave at 5:30 p.m., and do it all over again the next day) is an easy personal decision, a not-so-easy social one. Neighbors ask, "You're going alone, just you and the dog?" Even my wife, an experienced mountaineer, wondered. "The Marble Mountains—it's such a drive: five hours to Mount Shasta City, then another hour and a half to the trailhead the next day. Count me out." Then she laid the ultimate caveat on my shoulders: "If something happens to Blazer, just keep going north on Interstate 5. You can build a good life in Oregon. Bend maybe. Or Washington—the San Juans. Just promise me you won't let him out of your sight. Remember what happened to Max." My business partner, quite an athlete himself, asked,

"So do you take a cell phone with you in case of emergency?" Brother Rob, ten years my junior, had been trashed too many times before and wanted no part of another one of my "ass buster" high-country trips. When I poked him verbally about tagging along for old times' sake, he said succinctly, "Can't. Work."

Entering a wilderness such as Marble Mountain on your own engenders a feeling of timelessness. Except for the trails, a line shack or two, and the grazing Herefords, the mountains, forests, and meadows probably look pretty much the way they did thousands of years ago. The constellations, near galactic neighbors, and the Milky Way arching in a phosphorescent band overhead certainly haven't changed. Being there brings the order of the universe back into focus. It also is remarkable to consider that this complex matrix of plants, rocks, soil, animals, and birds, and dynamic weather functions in exquisite equilibrium without a single microprocessor.

For many people, solo wilderness travel (by that I mean without another human being) not only sharpens the senses, it intensifies the transition from civilization to wilderness. Few people can move from, say, downtown San Francisco, with all its conveniences and ordered chaos, to the backcountry of the John Muir Wilderness without a twinge or two of anxiety about marauding predators, violent weather, getting lost, or sustaining a debilitating injury. For me, dogs have pretty much taken care of the fear of predators. With a good dog curled up at my feet, the blackness at the edge of the campfire light loses its menace. I know that my canine companion will process the sound of that snapping twig at two o'clock in the morning and pronounce it ordinary or threatening by either remaining silent, barking, growling, or using body language. These dogs are like little foreign guides who live in cities but retain the language and customs of their rural brethren: the way a Pashtun from Kabul, Afghanistan, would interact on your behalf with hill tribes of Paktia.

Once the mantle of preoccupations and anxieties woven from a complex world of computers, digital data, instantaneous satellite telecommunications, microwaves, gridlock traffic, a vertiginous stock market, demanding clients, and electronic smog drops away, a sense of primal silence and wildness seeps into you. John Muir had it right when he wrote, "Climb the mountains and get their good tidings. Nature's peace will flow into you as sunshine flows into trees. The winds will blow their own freshness into you, and the storms their energy, while cares will drop off like autumn leaves."

From all except my wife, I sense an unstated question: "What do you do out there? No VCR, no FAX, no phone, no laptop, no TV, no pager, no instant messaging." A knee-jerk answer would be that getting unplugged from VCRs, Faxes, phones, laptops, TVs, pagers, instant messaging, voice mail, and personal digital assistants is reward enough in itself. Nor will I miss dodging the kamikaze bike messengers who delight in missing you by mere inches, playing crosswalk roulette with impatient city drivers, enduring eardrum-shredding emergency vehicles, avoiding persistent and malodorous panhandlers, seeing graffiti sprayed on buildings by mindless cretins, or sidestepping vomit splatters on the pavement. No, the hustle and the bustle will not be missed.

But getting unplugged is only part of the answer the uninitiated flatlanders seek. They want to know what it is that occupies a person's time out there. Well, how about watching the night sky develop over the rim of the world like a finely drawn etching; or scanning overhead for the first point of light from a magnitude one star or a planet, and then watching the constellations ignite one by one—Ursus Major, Ursus Minor, Cassiopeia, Leo, the summer triangle, the Pleiades: the polychromatic celestial host that affirms precision and constancy in the universe. How about holding a hot cup of tea in your hand at timberline in some far-flung wilderness while alpenglow fades from the highest spires, making them shine like sword tips fresh from the blacksmith's forge. Then there's the Thoreau-like satisfaction of distilling life to its simplest elements consistent with safety and a reasonable level of comfort: carrying all your needs on your back and drawing from the natural surroundings only water and wood for an occasional fire.

Early morning light reveals the mischief of

a night visitor; a chipmunk chewed my boot-
laces into three pieces, each of which I then
must painstakingly knot together before we hit
the trail for home. A flock of perky little songbirds about the size of canaries twitters away in
the red fir branches over our tent. Searching for
a likely dead tree full of grubs, a flicker flashes a
brown-and-white trajectory through the trees.
Even at this early hour, the day has a frisky feel
about it: lighter and less humid than yesterday—
more like fall. A light breeze from the north
probes the branches of fir trees and corrugates
the surface of Frying Pan Lake.

The isolation and privacy of this broad
ridge are well worth the price of having to haul
sixteen pounds of drinking water two hundred
yards from Frying Pan Lake twice a day. Last
night, high-pitched laughter echoing up from
a campsite at Lower Sky High Lake led me to
speculate that a group of girls in their early
teens probably were camped along the shoreline. Sure enough, this morning I hear distant
chatter, then spot them a quarter mile away
hiking with packs past Frying Pan Lake toward
the Pacific Crest Trail: four young girls led by
an adult female. They are oblivious to our presence. A German shepherd wearing saddlebags
walks off lead fifth in line like a docile pack
animal. I could no more trust Blazer off lead
than I could a wild coyote. In ten minutes he
would crest the ridge; in an hour he'd be in the
next county.

After breakfast, I begin to pack for the

journey home, slowed by a reluctance to leave this beautiful vantage point. Soon we are making our way north and a little east down the broad back of the moraine through high grass on a compass azimuth that should intersect the Sky High Valley Trail in a third of a mile. More than once I hoist Blazer by the strap on his pack like a piece of luggage to help him negotiate the stiff grass, which is knee high to me but over his head. He struggles through it with an expression of grim determination on his face mixed with a perverse glee at coming to grips with and defeating another obstacle thrown in his way.

Sooner than I expected, the ridge drops us onto the dusty trail, and we follow it downhill into the cool timber. Right off the bat Blazer starts his Iditarod routine, making me do the lambada over rocks and roots in the tread of the trail. It is time to put a halt to this foolishness. With full knowledge that rarely can you teach an old dog new tricks, I yank the leash back, forcing him behind me. At the same time I say, "Trace, Blaze. Trace!" For the first few hundred yards he tries to force his way past, first on my left, then on my right. Nothing doing. When my commands lose some effectiveness, I use a little switch on his nose. A few swats keep him back where I want him: about eighteen inches behind the heel of my boot. After a mile we're doing pretty well as a team. On the flats and uphill stretches, I call out, "Hup!" and he trots

ahead to the full length of the German-made
retractable leash. A sharp "trace" sends him back
to the rear. Thus my knee joints survive the
descent to the trailhead at Lover's Camp.

Angling in from the right a third of a mile
from the parking lot, we encounter the Red
Rock Valley Trail again, the fork we took two
days ago at the beginning of the trip. Visions
of a steaming spa at the Tree House Motel in
Mt. Shasta City; prawns sautéed in garlic with
Basmati rice, and a nice crisp salad of baby
greens with a light vinaigrette dressing at
Michael's Restaurant; a Sierra Nevada Pale Ale
so cold that condensation slides in rivulets
down the side of the bottle begin to form in
my mind's eye. Just as I quicken my pace, the
taut leash jerks me to the right, almost bowling
me over. I glance at Blazer to see him locked in
a classic hunting pose directed straight down
the fork to the Red Rock Valley Trail. After
twenty-plus miles, the eleven-year-old dog
wants to go around just one more time.
Brittanys.

Through the foresight of the citizenry, codified by the Mill Valley
General Plan, ridge tops in my hometown for the most part have
been left in their natural state. This network of oaks, madrone,
chinquapin, bay laurel, and chaparral represents a veritable highway for all kinds of wildlife, including cougars and feral pigs. It

is not uncommon, for instance, to see a silver gray fox curled up in a ball on Joe Scafidi's driveway across the street, contentedly soaking up the early morning sun. A wild turkey may saunter brazenly down our street in the morning. Rarely does a night pass without an opossum, skunk, or raccoon shuffling provocatively by the kitchen door, sending Blazer into a frenzy of barking. We always keep Blazer on a short lead when we traverse the fire road at the top of Blithedale Ridge where a breeding pair of cougars has taken up residence.

Early one morning while Blazer and I were walking along the Bob Middagh Trail, a path that slices east-west across a steep meadow above our house, an agitated doe burst out of the brush and charged downhill toward the baffled dog, kicked at him with a sharp hind hoof, and sprinted around the ridge. The attack so unnerved the Brittany that he turned around, retraced his steps, and returned home at a good clip. I found him waiting for me on the front deck.

Other ambushers are closer to the ground. Take skunks, for instance. Most encounters with skunks occurred on walks at night when the flashlight beam slicing though the bushes along the road would spotlight a white-and-black fuzz ball. Jerking the leash back with the right timing usually was enough to check Blazer's headlong rush into malodorous catastrophe. The night he got nailed was closer to home. He had just turned the corner of the house on his way to a pre-bedtime pee in the backyard when a vagrant skunk ambling through cut loose and caught him square in the face and chest with a stream of foul-smelling liquid. Neither Claire nor I noticed anything amiss when he scooted back around the corner, through the kitchen, and into the living room. But the extent of the disaster became abundantly clear when we ran into a wall of choking stench ballooning out from the living room where Blazer desperately was trying to rub off the suffocating oil by rolling and rooting around on the carpet. I grabbed him by the collar and led him back into the kitchen while Claire rushed to prepare her secret anti-skunk formula: a

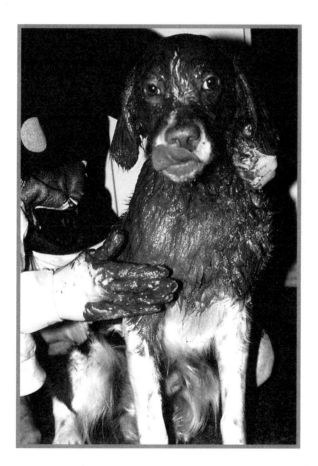

paste of nonfat dried milk, instant coffee, and water mixed to the consistency of pancake batter. The trick is to smear it on the affected parts of the Brittany's coat, then wait for forty-five minutes to an hour while the dog reflexively licks off the paste within range of his tongue. This late-night setback carried us well past bedtime—in fact, pushing midnight. When we finally settled in, the bedroom was redolent with a whiff of skunk laced with coffee: as if Pepe LePew had ordered a double latte no whip at Starbucks and then got flattened by a semi.

My hunt for a more effective essence-de-skunk neutralizer led me to the Marin County Humane Society. They suggested I call Burton Butler, the "skunk expert." Over the phone one rainy afternoon, Burton sounded like an affable and informative man who, it turned out, lives in my hometown of Mill Valley. You hear about advocates for all sorts of wildlife, from three-toed salamanders to cougars to spotted owls. But how did he get to be the Saint Francis of Assisi for skunks? He told me he had worked with animals a lot and for many years was on the board of WildCare, a wildlife rehabilitation and education center in San Rafael.

I told Burton about several noxious Brittany-skunk encounters we'd had and asked him if he would give me his best formula for neutralizing skunk spray. He said, "That business about tomato juice was made up by the tomato juice companies. It doesn't work. We got a good formula from the chemical companies: One quart of hydrogen peroxide, a quarter cup of baking soda, and a teaspoon of dishwashing liquid. Wash the dog as you normally would, using the formula as a shampoo. The dissipated smell will remain for a while, but the skunk spray itself will have been neutralized. If the spray hits your clothing, don't try to wash it. Throw it out. Along with the hydrogen-peroxide formula, ionizers work great in houses and in closets. The ionizer will take the smell right out of clothes. The ionizer literally cleans the air to where it smells sort of like after the first rain. It pumps the molecules and cleans up the air. I use something called Living Air. You can find it on the Internet. Ionizers are expensive, but they work."

Blazer's most disastrous encounter with wildlife occurred when he was less than a year old. One evening he acted lethargic, had no appetite or energy, and hyperventilated a lot. The vet was so concerned about his condition that she kept him overnight for observation. The next day, she informed Claire that he had clusters of ulcers on the roof of his mouth and possibly down his throat. She was not certain of the origin, but speculated that insects might have caused them. Blazer was so dehydrated that she had him on intravenous fluids. When he returned home four days later, he was thinner, almost gaunt. His prescription included lots of chicken soup as a way to keep him hydrated. What puzzled us was the vague diagnosis. Insects?

A few days later I was scuffing through the leaves beneath the Lombardy poplar tree in our backyard when I heard a muffled humming sound and a faint vibration in the ground. Thanks to what I had learned during my early experiences as a seasonal forest firefighter in the deep woods of Oregon, I scurried up the hill and around the corner. Soon I was back, looking like a cross between a mad professor of anthropology and Jack Armstrong, the astronaut. I was wearing a hard hat with a mosquito net pulled over it and tucked into the collar of my Gore-Tex mountain parka. The cuffs of my jeans were duct-taped shut over the tops of my boots. I wore thick gloves and a sturdy long-sleeved shirt, and I carried the biggest can of Ortho hornet spray I could find.

The first phase of my attack on this ground nest of yellow jackets (which I was convinced had attacked Blazer and cost us several hundred dollars in vet bills) was a barrage of smoke from a gopher gasser. I lit the fuse, dropped the stick into the small opening of the hive, and tamped some dirt over the entrance with my boot. The intensity of what happened next took me by surprise. The subterranean hive began to vibrate with the energy of several hundred enraged yellow jackets gunning their engines and spinning their propellers in a frantic bid to escape the gas attack. The noise grew louder in pulses, like a generator straining to keep up with an overloaded electrical system. The few stalwart insects that managed to claw their way through the loose dirt near the entrance died in a lethal stream of Ortho. Soon the battlefield was littered with soggy corpses. Smoke from the gopher gasser curled up from the seething soil. The humming diminished and then faded out. Blazer's revenge was complete.

Unlike Max—whose Alpha dog wiring often got him into trouble when he would taunt and dare other dogs until we had a fight on our hands—Blazer, with his gentle personality, was guaranteed to be the attackee rather than the attacker. A mugging that occurred during a hike on Mount Tamalpais one Sunday was a classic example.

By the time we had parked the Jeep at the trailhead and chugged halfway up a steep fire trail toward the rocky spine of Blithedale Ridge, the remnant storm clouds had evaporated, leaving the country resplendent in afternoon sun spilling over the summit of the mountain. The air was sweet with ceanothus, Douglas iris, suncups, and lupine. It was the glorious break we had been waiting for in a relentless cycle of El Niño storms. Claire, thin as a reed after a bout with pneumonia, strode up the trail at her brisk backcountry pace behind Blazer, who was nine years old at the time. Some years before, an unleashed out-of-control dog had attacked Blazer, wrenching his back. I was just recovering from a recent back injury myself.

Thus, our trio of wounded adventurers topped the ridge and began hiking northwest along the rocky fire road, absorbing the last rays of the sun. Silhouetted by the oblique sunlight, a woman and a dog appeared at a bend in the trail ahead of us. The dog, a nondescript yellow Labrador retriever weighing about seventy-five pounds, ambled ahead of her while she sauntered along with a short leather lead draped around her neck. As the dog approached Blazer, the woman called out, "Oh, he's so muddy. I hope he doesn't get your dog dirty. He's so clean looking."

Not two seconds after she said that, her lab jumped

Blazer, glommed on to his neck, and began mauling his thirty-six-pound body unmercifully. The attack was as unprovoked as it was unexpected. Blazer's legs went out from under him, and the meat-grinder jaws of the enraged lab began to do their work. It was as if Mike Tyson had decided to use Woody Allen as a speed bag. I grabbed the lab by his collar, hoisted him up chest high, and began hauling him up the fire road. Suspended by his neck, the dog thrashed around frantically, smearing my Royal Robbins trousers with adobe mud. Cursing, I swung him in an arc, and he flew out of his collar.

As the woman clipped him into the leash, I yelled, "What the hell is going on? Haven't you heard of the Marin County leash law? If he's dangerous, he should be on a leash or under voice control!"

"He's never done that before. I don't know why he did that."

"Oh, right! We've heard that one before. You can't tell me he hasn't jumped other dogs before!"

"Is your dog injured?" she asked.

"I don't know. The last time this happened, he seemed OK. Two hours later, his back seized up. The vet bill was $600, and we never got the dog owner's name. I appreciate your concern, but why didn't you keep your dog under control?"

Although his ears were all gummed up and he seemed dazed and embarrassed, there was no blood on Blazer's cinnamon-and-cream coat. The dogs eyeballed each other warily.

"A lot of people walk their dogs off leash along this section of the ridge," the woman said. "You might consider walking him near Homestead Valley. There's a place over there where everyone keeps their dogs on leashes. Maybe he won't get attacked then."

"He wouldn't have gotten attacked if you had control of your dog. We're not litigious people, but sooner or later that dog is going to land you in deep doo doo."

About that time, Claire waded in with some choice words she reserves for those who abuse animals, kids, and old people. Probably sensing that things were spinning out of control and the time had come to beat a tactical retreat, the woman offered a telephone number and asked us to call if Blazer required veterinary attention.

Now stoked with fear and loathing instead of tranquility and a sense of natural beauty, we climbed the ridge in a sullen funk. Claire was literally shaking with anxiety and anger. I reeled off a litany of other attacks we'd experienced in the past few years.

Two black labs the size of Volkswagens attacked one afternoon, dragging their owner, a middle-aged woman, behind them along the trail by Salt Creek. Her story was—surprise, surprise—the dogs had never attacked before, so something about Blazer must have provoked them.

A large mixed breed being walked off lead by a tall, elderly man along the bike trail behind Lucky Market jumped

Blazer during our Sunday morning run. The owner's excuse for the attack was that I didn't give him time enough to grab his dog (he didn't even carry a leash!). I stuck to him like a winter tick, unloading on him about his irresponsible habits while he struggled along for half a mile bent over, holding the dog by its collar. He refused to identify himself so I gave his license plate number to the Mill Valley Police Department.

Another mixed breed attacked Blazer at Shoreline Park one Sunday while we were on an early morning run. The clueless couple apologized but never identified themselves. This was the attack that left us six hundred dollars poorer from the vet bill for Blazer's wrenched back; we wished we had dragged the couple by the scruffs of their necks over to the nearby Public Safety Building and had them booked for felony ignorance and stupidity.

Claire's Precious Little Man, her Budmeister, her Precious Angel, Blazer turned out to be a combination of Red and Max in personality, if not physical characteristics. She thought he was more responsive and snuggly and less assertive and rambunctious than Max. Yet he acted like Red in many ways. Before contracting chronic rhinitis, he had been a pretty good bird hunter. What he lacked in territorial awareness (he often blundered into adjacent fields, drawing angry responses from other hunters) he made up for in enthusiasm and innate proficiency. A major failing was his aversion to fetching. The best he could force himself to do was to pursue downed birds across the soggy fields, pin them against some brush, and then proceed to pluck their tail feathers out with this front teeth. Perhaps his higher calling would have been as a feather plucker in the back room of the hunting lodge.

One cameo performance happened on a bright November day at Suisun Marsh Hunting Preserve while we were traversing a field long after most hunters had called it quits. I wanted to work Blazer a little longer to steady up his points and refine his response to my commands. He was quartering across the dry stubble about fifteen yards in front of me when he froze in as perfect a point as I could expect for that stage of his development: right front paw curled back stylishly, back as straight as a carpenter level, eyes locked on a clump of grass. About that time,

Roy Saucerman, the manager of the preserve, rolled down the levee in his pickup truck. He stopped and cranked down the window to observe. As I edged slowly past Blazer, Remington Model 870 12-gauge at the ready, a fat cock pheasant burst up out of the grass and started propelling itself out of range. The first shot staggered him and the second brought him down. Blazer hadn't moved until the bird nosed over into a dive.

Roy yelled out of the window, "He's lookin' pretty sharp, there. How old is he?"

"About a year and a half," I responded, beaming at Blazer's timely performance. What I didn't tell Roy was that I was hoarse from yelling at the dog continuously as we had worked the edge of a drainage canal. He kept ranging out too far, ignoring my commands, until we maneuvered our way into the flat by the road and Roy showed up.

Blazer's second hunting season was a disaster. He refused to listen to commands and kept ranging way out in front of the hunting party, trespassing onto adjacent fields. We resorted to a long trailing rope clipped to his collar, but it kept getting snagged on limbs and brush. It was obvious he thought he knew more about the sport than we did. The next step would have been electrotherapy: shock collar training at Black Point Sports Club under a trainer with a reputation for firmness, but somehow the opportunity never presented itself. It also became a moot point after Blazer contracted the chronic rhinitis that degraded his olfactory system. His hunting days were over.

Blazer's worsening condition prompted Claire to take him to the local vet. Antibiotics had little effect on reducing the ropy lime-green discharge that erupted from his nose with each explosive sneeze: if you've ever seen a squashed banana slug, then you've got the idea. The next stop was the Mayo Clinic for animals: the Veterinary Medical Teaching Hospital at the University of California at Davis. Four days of diagnostic tests left the vets scratching their heads about the exact agent causing the allergy. Blazer returned home with prescriptions for prednisone, phenylpropanolamine, and chlorpheniramine stapled to a sizeable bill. Beconase spray (prescribed for humans with allergies) and glucocorticoid spray were backups in case the first battery of pharmaceuticals didn't work.

His rhinitis improved at first. Then a few weeks later he regressed into the old pattern. Worse, the drugs were turning him into a hyperactive insomniac. One night he was so frantic to escape his kennel in the kitchen, he pulled down the oven door with his front paws and used it as a trampoline to vault through the opening into the living room and ultimately into our bedroom. The wear and tear on him and on our sleep had to stop. In desperation, Claire contacted an animal behaviorist. Along with her assessment of Blazer's condition, the behaviorist recommended Dr. Stan Goldfarb, an associate at the East San Rafael Veterinary Clinic in a small community to the north of us. The behaviorist told us that Dr. Goldfarb was a traditional veterinarian with expertise in solving some health problems using homeopathic remedies. He calls himself the Home Vet.

I accompanied Claire on her first visit to the clinic, a modest one-story building with small examining rooms off a main hallway. Dr. Goldfarb, a wiry, intense-looking man in his fifties, introduced himself and began the treatment by unpacking a case containing labeled glass vials. He explained that they contained a variety of substances, including vitamins, minerals, foods, vaccines, bacteria, molds, viruses, pollens, pesticides, chemicals, pharmaceuticals, toxic metals, and flea and heartworm medications. He would use a theory of "surrogate transfer" of sensitivity to these substances to arrive at a treatment protocol designed to lessen the symptoms and make life more comfortable for Blazer. As the months rolled on, Blazer's anxiety faded and his rhinitis diminished to a manageable level. We realized Dr. Goldfarb had succeeded where a traditional vet and the experts at Davis had failed.

Goldfarb then expanded the nontraditional treatment to Blazer's perennial back problem, the legacy of the attack by an unleashed dog. We thought the injury was responsible for gradual atrophy in the muscles of his right rear leg. Some months before, I had noticed him for the first time struggling to climb a set of stairs in the backyard. On Dr. Goldfarb's advice, Claire began taking Blazer to monthly treatments by Michael Gleason, a chiropractic specialist from Tracy, California, who worked with the clinic. As an adjunct to Gleason's conventional chiropractic techniques, Dr. Goldfarb used a system of lighted needles, called

Microstim, on Blazer's back. The consequence of this regimen of treatments was that all of Blazer's conditions became manageable. His nasal discharges no longer were a threat to life and limb. He slept comfortably through the night, forged ahead during walks, and took the backyard stairs two at a time. Not bad for twelve years old, roughly equivalent to sixty-three years in a human.

Those days, Blazer and I commiserated about the afflictions of middle age. Arthroscopic surgery on my knee the year before and his degenerative nerve condition had taken us both out of the running, so to speak. But we still walked for half an hour in the hills after work each day and longer on the weekends. Cross-country skiing was still a viable alternative, as was paddling about in a canoe or a sea kayak. He was getting better treatment than most older people with the usual infirmities of aging. Dr. Goldfarb had him on a special diet of raw hamburger (Claire insisted on buying the finest grade sirloin), cooked vegetables, a starch, Vitamin C, a dry kibble called PHD, and a plethora of natural supplements like fish oil capsules, glucosamine and chondroitin sulfate for his joints, a powder called Transfer Factor for rhinitis, and some other amendments to combat anxiety, fatigue, and problems of the immune system.

We first noticed Blazer had developed an asymmetric gait when his toenail started bleeding after an hour walk through the upscale neighborhood of Strawberry. On closer inspection, we noticed he was favoring his right rear leg by allowing the foot to "knuckle under" and scrape along the asphalt. I recommended using his rubber hunting boots fastened with stretchy athletic tape from a medical supply house until we could get a handle on this new infirmity. Dr. Goldfarb and his chiropractic associate, Michael Gleason, suspected a loss of muscle mass. The interim solution was physical resistance therapy—laying him on his back twice a day and "pumping" or "bicycling" his rear legs twenty times. Claire, the overachiever, started out at twenty, soon ratcheted it up to thirty-five, and then to forty. She ended up at over three hundred times per session, thereby slowing the rate loss of muscle mass considerably. After pumping his legs, Claire draped a special pad she had heated in the microwave oven across Blazer's back. It exuded an exotic aroma of rosemary and other herbs, and was designed to stimulate circulation. But what was causing this degenerative condition? We had no clue and neither did the veterinarians.

In February 2000, we followed Stan Goldfarb's advice and drove Blazer up the road to the Small Animal Clinic in Rohnert Park to consult with Vince Pedroia, a noted animal neurologist. This would be the last stop before taking him to Davis. Pedroia turned out to be a tall, athletic-looking man in his late forties who had a professional air about him and listened well. He told us the diagnostic phase would involve a trip to Santa Rosa Hospital for a battery of tests, including a CT-scan, so we would have to leave Blazer with him for a few days. When we returned to his office on a rainy Friday afternoon, Pedroia told us his diagnosis—neuropathy or degeneration of the nerves serving the muscles of the leg. The cause was inconclusive, though Pedroia's prime suspect was old age. His previous theories, cancerous tumors on the spine or damage to a disc from the attack at Shoreline Park some years ago, evaporated when the test results came in. "When dogs get to this age," he observed, "most people put them down." Then he made the unhappy prediction that Blazer wouldn't last six months. Dr. Pedroia didn't realize that Claire's hackles tend to rise and adrenalin starts to flow when those close to her are threatened. She was far from ready to give up on the old guy. As I would observe later, she was just beginning to fight. Pedrioia's assistant brought out a stinky, groggy Brittany with matted hair and dye marks on his legs. He was weak and wobbly from a sedative, so she was steering him from behind by the tail. We wrapped him in towels and put him in the car. On the drive back down Highway 101 to Mill Valley after settling a $2000 bill, Claire observed, "You don't put your grandfather down just because he has to use a cane. Why put down a dog just because he's getting along in years?" We both vowed to keep Blazer going as long as he wanted to keep going; we would accommodate his infirmities to the degree possible, keep him comfortable, and above all let him know we had not given up on him. The signal to shut down would have to come from him.

"The benchmark should be when he can't get out of bed in the morning," said Claire. "Even he would agree that a Brittany's life is pretty much over when that happens. Until then, we'll do everything possible to keep him going, as long as his

never-say-die attitude and stamina. Stan attributed it to our dedication. We attributed it to Stan's professionalism.

One Sunday morning Claire thought she detected another step down. Just short of a mile along the bike-walk path at Blackie's Pasture, Blazer did a U-turn and headed back toward the truck. "This is it," Claire thought. "Now he's shortening the walks." A bit dejected, she followed him back to the parking lot. To her surprise, he pulled her past the truck and up the road westbound toward the Presbyterian Church and Lyford House, an historical structure by the bay—a new and interesting direction. To her great relief and joy, she realized that he had just gotten bored with the regular walk.

We had noticed this proclivity about a year before, on walks around the neighborhood. It turned out that in typical

Brittany fashion he was just seeking new adventures, fresh venues, mental stimulation, something beyond the ordinary. I started conjuring up new routes to keep him challenged. Blazer responded by forging ahead and acting more excited and interested. But as soon as we merged with the old routes, he balked or turned around. We thought flat trails would be more to his liking, given his geriatric condition. To the contrary, for some reason he preferred the more demanding and strenuous routes like the Secret Trail, a dark path that twists radically up through deep woods of bay laurel. It was only a glorified deer trail, but it always got his juices flowing. At the top of Horse Hill, it breaks out of a grove of bay laurel trees into a meadow. Blazer loved it, even though it taxed his dwindling physical reserves. The snorting, grazing horses we often encountered there fascinated him.

On a Wednesday afternoon Claire was walking Blazer along Sunnyside Drive in Mill Valley when they passed a gaggle of teenagers. As usual, Blazer was wearing his orthopedic boots. One of the teenagers—apparently the leader—snickered to his friends as they passed by. Claire locked them up with her famous "stink eye" for a few seconds, then explained to the clueless boys that Blazer was the canine equivalent of an 85-year-old. He suffered from muscle weakness due to a nerve disorder. The boots were to protect his feet from the rough concrete. Just hope someone takes such good care of you when you get this old. Any questions? Nope.

Having figured Blazer out, Claire tried to keep him

interested by doing the Blackie's Pasture route in reverse. Regardless, he continued to lose muscle mass. Stan told her it was normal at his age, but prescribed homeopathic compounds designed to rebuild muscle. When Blazer could no longer negotiate the stairs leading to the second floor of our home, where he relished the daily ritual of "cocktail cookies" in my office after the walk, I helped him with a gentle boost under his butt. As the months passed, he had increasing difficulty negotiating other obstacles, such as the stairs from the lower terrace of the backyard. He began to choose the gentler east path rather than the main stairs, and to spend most of his day in the Brittany condo or the pebbled walkway next to it. We ramped the entrance to his hatch and later ramped the steps from the pavers, being careful not to insult his Brittany hubris by babying him or being overly attentive. Regardless of our doting presence, he usually preferred to have a run at an obstacle himself before accepting assistance. After a typical afternoon walk, I would grab a beer and some munchies, then head to my second-floor office to tackle paperwork. At first, Blazer tried to follow me up the stairs, but he collapsed at the bottom after several feeble attempts that made him cry in frustration. Often he would make another run at it and succeed. Sheer guts.

One morning Claire noticed his bladder had released overnight in his "Double Doughnut" bed. Fortunately, the design of this Duxiana of dog beds allowed for easy removal of the pad and cover for washing. To further neutralize the problem, she bought denim pants with Velcro sides designed for bitches in heat. The liner that comes with the pants was a little wimpy, so Claire used Pampers as liners. Feminine napkins with extra-long wings also worked well, giving more lateral protection. Thus, she solved the nocturnal incontinence problem: one more strategy for living with a senior Brittany you're not yet ready to give up. Meals, walks, and cocktail hour still were the highlights of his day.

If you interact with your Brittany as you should, taking him on a walk at least once a day, invariably these little ambassadors will introduce you not only to neighbors but to distant cousins of theirs you might not care to meet. Take canis latrans, the real-life model for the cartoon character Wile E. Coyote. One Saturday we were unloading groceries from the truck in the driveway when Claire complained, "Just listen to those coyotes! Now they're howling in broad daylight. Next they'll be hanging around the kitchen for handouts. I don't like it. They give me the creeps. Why don't they just go somewhere else?"

Sure enough, one of the characters was raising hell in a ravine next to Salt Creek, on the edge of Alto Bowl not far from the Scott Valley Swim and Tennis Club. But he wasn't howling; it was more like yapping: barking and high-pitched squealing. I had heard this guy some weeks before during an evening walk with Blazer along the fire road next to Salt Creek and wondered what prompted the outburst. Since Blazer was almost 14 and his hearing was shot, he wasn't any help at all. It was a year earlier that I first heard the coyotes singing on the ridge of Horse Hill. Their serenade, waxing and waning on the night air, evoked the sheer exuberance of hunting, the beauty of the platinum moonlight spilling across the meadows, the freedom of the hills, the synergy of the nomadic pack. To me, it was thrilling to hear a sound I associated with the high country. But they made Claire nervous, with some justification it turns out.

In February, Cassie, a white Bichon Frise, disappeared from her home at the base of Horse Hill. Later in the day, the owner looked up and saw a coyote standing over some object in the grass. The man's approach frightened the animal away and revealed the mangled body of poor Cassie. During a walk through the neighborhood with Blazer one evening, I encountered the owner of Hanna, the Welsh springer spaniel that was Blazer's ultimate heartthrob. While the dogs titillated each other shamelessly, Hanna's owner told me that one summer evening Hanna had wandered up the flank of Horse Hill. At the very moment her owner was calling her in, two coyotes raced downhill and rolled Hanna head over heels in the oat grass. Her escape, facilitated by the owner's frantic yelling, was nothing short of miraculous.

This relatively recent appearance of new predators close to home piqued my curiosity about whether it was common to have them living so close to developed areas and prompted me to learn more about the animal Mark Twain called "the most friendless of God's creatures." About ten square kilometers will sustain an average family of coyotes, which at its largest consists of a male and female (often mated for life, which typically lasts for six to eight years) and a litter of pups. Coyotes breed around January, and seven to nine dark gray pups arrive about two months later. To accommodate the litter, the adults dig dens five to thirty feet deep or occupy hollow logs, culverts, or dens abandoned by other animals. An omnivorous opportunist, a coyote will eat rodents, birds, frogs, toads, insects, snakes, garbage, fruit, berries, road kill, and sometimes larger animals such as fawns. Camilla Fox (her real name), national campaign director for the Animal Protection Institute, told me that widespread attempts to control coyote populations have had little long-term impact because the coyotes' strong compensatory responses such as increased litter sizes and pup survival allow them to replenish their numbers and reoccupy vacated habitats. When lethal control produces a short-term reduction of a coyote population, coyotes immigrating from surrounding areas soon fill the vacuum. Fox also said that coyotes which have been habituated to human activity (most often as the result of people intentionally or unintentionally feeding them) can likewise be trained to fear humans again through aversive conditioning techniques. By that she meant confronting coyotes that are encroaching on developed areas by yelling at them or throwing sticks and small clods of earth (to strike the body, not the head).

The city of Glendale, California, instituted a model

coexistence program after problems with coyotes developed in 1981, problems precipitated by citizens who made a habit of sitting in lawn chairs and watching coyotes eat hand-delivered food. The Glendale police captain, Michael Post, was quoted as saying, "The prevalent scientific view prescribes educated coexistence as the only realistic long-term solution of coyote–human conflicts." So what to do in Marin County where we live? Camilla Fox and other experts suggested that some of the following approaches might lead to coexistence:

- Secure your garbage cans, and don't leave garbage out overnight; put it out on the morning of pick-up.
- Keep ripe fruit off the ground.
- Install outdoor lights with motion detectors.
- Never attempt to tame or feed a coyote.
- Instill fear in encroaching coyotes by making loud noises or throwing objects at their bodies, not their heads.
- Keep cats and dogs indoors at night.
- Don't leave pet food or water bowls outside.

On a nightly walk with Blazer, I got to test the aversive conditioning technique I had been reading about when a medium-sized coyote trotted across the road and sat down in a mini meadow, watching us. I shined the beam of a flashlight in his eyes and charged full-tilt toward him, yelling and stomping my feet. Blazer hobbled along behind, his orthopedic rubber boots going putt-putt-putt on the asphalt. Sure enough, the startled animal turned tail and scooted across the meadow into the French broom.

September and October are golden months at Lake Tahoe in California's Sierra Nevada Mountains. Indian Summer sometimes lingers into late October, then dissipates before the armada of Pacific storms that pummels the crest with snow through late April. Short vacations during the pause between the tourist-jammed summer and the skier-jammed winter find the pace slower, roads practically empty, restaurants uncrowded. Swaths of amber and gold leaves splashing across granite slopes herald freezing nights and calm, shirtsleeve days. At this stage of Blazer's life, devising a way to take him with us on outdoor ventures was a difficult challenge. Neuropathy and arthritis limited the range of his walks. Since we normally brought our mountain bikes on these short vacations, we decided one way to get him out into his beloved fresh air and open country was to buy a bike trailer and customize it with Ensolite pads for his bony body. Recreational Equipment Incorporated (REI) sold us a one-wheel BOB Yak trailer for around three hundred bucks; I rationalized that I could also use it to haul equipment and food for an extended bike expedition in the future. Manufactured out of aluminum tubing, it locks to the rear wheel hub and obediently trails along behind.

At thirty pounds, Blazer didn't challenge the payload maximum of seventy pounds.

One crisp autumn morning we drove to Squaw Valley,

spectacular venue for the VIII Winter Olympic Games in 1960. We hooked the trailer to my Trek mountain bike, helped Blazer into it, fastened our helmets, and took off along a bike and walking path that parallels the old railroad right-of-way along the banks of the Truckee River. On the way to Tahoe City and back, a distance of around nine miles, we stopped frequently to let Blazer stretch his legs, sample the river water, smell the sedges and alder trees, and watch mallards and mergansers flap away across the rapids. Our cruising pace of about twelve miles an hour afforded Blazer an opportunity to savor a slipstream that was laced with tantalizing fragrances. The look on his graying face was all the reward we needed.

Joey

Our Resident Senior, as Claire fondly called Blazer, entered his fifteenth year with the expected age-related infirmities: loose and unpredictable bowels and bladder, chronic rhinitis, neuropathy in his hindquarters, and failing eyesight and hearing. Despite his age and condition, the Brittany spirit burned bright in his soul: meal times and "walkies" in the hills still made his day. Sunday morning sojourns with Claire along the Tiburon bike path from Blackie's Pasture prompted questions from other walkers curious to know the reason for the boots. Some sniggered among themselves about "little booties on the dog," to which Claire continued to assert politely but firmly, "They're orthopedic boots, not a fashion statement. He's fifteen. He has neuropathy."

Mindful of the fact that Blazer's weekdays were spent in his condo in the basement, with occasional trips outside to answer nature's call, Claire decided he needed a companion to buffer the loneliness and distract him from his infirmities. While acutely conscious of her ambivalence about finding a young companion for Blazer (would he sink into depression, or draw energy and enthusiasm from the youngster?), Claire surfed the American Brittany Rescue (ABR) Web site, www.americanbrittanyrescue.org, for likely candidates. More than once I found her teary-eyed in front of the monitor, clicking through poignant tales of abandoned, sick, and injured dogs, especially the seniors. Would Blazer feel neglected, she wondered, if we brought a younger dog aboard and brought him up to speed with obedience training and house rules? In late September, she told me about an interesting prospect. Although Lucky looked a little goofy, she was intrigued by his proximity—a foster home only a mile away from us in Mill Valley. What would it hurt, I asked her on Friday, just to take a peek at him: no prior commitments, just an inspection visit? Somewhat reluctantly, she called the foster—an attorney named David—who agreed to bring him over on Saturday while Claire was at her morning aerobics class. I would let her know if, by our standards, Lucky passed first muster. Then we both could check him out on Sunday.

When I opened the door to David's knock on Saturday, I sensed we had a new dog. Lucky had the build of a marathoner—long powerful legs, big feet, a deep chest, and well-muscled hindquarters. At three and a half years old, he appeared to be on the gaunt side of healthy. His flat coat was a glowing patchwork of bright ivory and rich mahogany. Most remarkable about him were his eyes. Like variegated amber set in a large square head,

they tracked me steadily as David followed ABR requirements
to inspect our house, the yard, and the Brittany condo in the
basement. "He was on death row at the Martinez Animal Shelter
when ABR called," David told me. "I just lost Partner, my fifteen-
year-old Brittany, this spring, so it was hard to turn them down.
But I'm not ready for another dog yet."

After David left, the phone rang. Claire had to know the
verdict, even though her class was still in session. "He's a keeper,"
I told her. "But you're the final judge." At dinner that night I
supplied more detail. David had told me Lucky was one of two
Brittanys abandoned at the Martinez Animal Shelter on the same
day, the other being his brother Tango. ABR learned that the
unfortunate dogs had spent their entire lives in a 7- by 11-foot
outside enclosure until the owner realized he would never have

the time to train them for bird hunting, so he dumped them at the shelter. The shelter staff thought Lucky had some aggressive tendencies and was making arrangements to put him down when ABR offered to take him and his brother. Still riddled with ambivalence, Claire drove with me to meet Lucky at David's house the next day. Later she would tell me that what hooked her was the sight of him peering intently out of David's den window, wagging his stump of a tail furiously as if to say, "Oh boy. These must be my new people." David told us that had he kept him, he would have changed his name to Joey—a moniker that better fit his personality and David's fondness for the movie Pal Joey. We adopted Joey on the spot and thanked David, who welled up a bit at saying goodbye to yet another Brittany, even though we promised him visitation rights.

Back home, introduction to Blazer went well, to judge by the tail wagging and polite sniffing. Still, I sensed Claire was having problems. Later she confessed to guilt feelings. Did she rush into this too soon? Would Blazer go into a funk? Was she being disloyal to the old guy after all these years of loyalty, companionship, and love? Is the adoption reversible? Her angst spiked that afternoon when Joey made a playful pass at Blazer, bowling him over on the living room rug. The old guy's howls of indignation and upside-down thrashing shook Claire's confidence in her judgment. "What have I done to my senior?" she asked. "Is this fair to him at his age?" Later, doubts, recriminations, and outright uncertainty kept her awake most of the night. I did what I could to assure her that Joey soon would settle down and become a positive factor in Blazer's life.

Meanwhile, as I was bringing extra water and food bowls in from the garage that evening for Joey's first meal with us, disaster struck. Claire opened the front door for me and Joey vaulted over Blazer, bolted through the opening, and threw a body block into me, knocking one of the bowls out of my hand. It tumbled to the deck and shattered. I swung back toward the driveway as quickly as I could, but he was gone into the black night. We called his name to no avail, even using the old moniker, Lucky. No response. Panic rose. "Call David and tell him to be on the lookout!" I yelled to Claire as I rushed out toward the street carrying a leash and a flashlight. "And you might as well alert the Mill Valley Police Department." Cones of light thrown from streetlights illuminated only parked cars. No Joey. I wracked my brain for likely destinations a dog in an unfamiliar neighborhood might choose. Finally, gut instinct prevailed. He's a hunter, I reasoned, so he's probably probing the ravines and meadows above our house that are redolent with deer, quail, and coyote spoor. A steep, narrow trail led me past Indian Rock—the cluster of boulders, bay laurel trees, and oaks that shelter Max's last resting place. The irony of searching for a runaway dog near the grave of a wild head who himself died running away was not lost on me. I turned right on a wider trail, the Bob Middagh, that traverses the meadow east toward Salt Creek. Calling his name, I followed my flashlight's oval glow as the trail cut left and dropped into the darkened ravine. A patch of white flashed, then disappeared behind a hedge of blackberries. It reappeared. It's got to be Joey or a skunk, I thought to myself. If there's a God in heaven, then let it be Joey. I called his name and moved closer. It disappeared again. After several minutes of this game, I concluded that since it was unlikely I would ever have gotten that far anyway, I had nothing to lose by using a desperate tactic. Keeping the flashlight low, I turned around and walked back up the hill while calling his name. "Let's go home, Lucky. Time to eat. That's a gooood boy. Come on." After ten yards, I looked back, and sure enough there was Joey, creeping up the trail. When I turned toward him, he stopped. I continued up the hill, followed by the anxious and confused dog. When the gap between us shrank to eight feet, I turned, kneeled, and put my hand out. "Good dog, Lucky. Cookies. Let's go home." He collapsed on the dusty trail. I snapped the lead on his collar and exhaled like a migrating humpback whale.

As one week rolled into another, the mantle of neglect and abuse that Joey wore on his arrival in our household began to slip off. Anxious whining at the garden gate during our absences diminished. Cowering and slinking away at my approach gave way to tail wagging and enthusiastic welcoming rituals. We soon realized Joey was a blank slate—a puppy trapped in the body of a three-year-old bird dog. It was obvious he had never been welcomed inside a house, walked on a lead, or offered food in his own bowl. He inhaled his meals like a ravenous hyena: forty seconds flat by my stopwatch, much to David's amusement when he stopped by for dinner one night. I told David I had never before seen a dog "eat" his water. Soon his prominent ribcage disappeared as he gained weight without altering his lanky, graceful physique. Even though he was a gangly guy with a big head and big feet, people stopped us on the street to remark about his handsome body and showy coat. The layers of inhibiting baggage continued to peel away, revealing a sweet, almost needy disposition, a clownish exuberance, fascination with

flying objects of any variety, a thirst for outdoor adventure, and an insatiable appetite for ripe blackberries.

Around the house Joey became a shadow, trailing Claire or me to the office, den, guest room, living room, kitchen, or laundry room. He even enjoyed watching me putter in the garage. He seemed fascinated by what we were doing and, most of all, seemed to want to make sure we didn't slip away never to return. He seemed starved for human contact and affection. When either one of us approached him, he dropped his head, collapsed upside down on the floor, and offered his chest for a rub. Often he crept into my office where I was trying to pay bills or write. He would lay his big head in my lap and then ever so tentatively raise his forequarters until we were eyeball-to-eyeball —not conducive to business or creativity but perhaps essential from his perspective, to solidify Brittany-human bonding.

When we were away from the house, Joey and Blazer shared the comfortable condo in the basement complete with

insulated kennels, fresh water, play toys, boiled bones, and carpeted surfaces. Classical music played from a radio in the corner. A hatch led to the multilevel yard that was perfect for high-speed cruising, stalking winter birds in the multiflora rose hedge, or watching buzzards cruise lazily over the meadows and clouds form over the shoulder of Mount Tamalpais. As the dry northwest winds of autumn conceded the stage to wet, southwest storms, Joey reinforced his relationship with Blazer and adapted to the household routine.

At times Claire wondered whether two dogs were one too many. While waiting for the Malugani guys on Miller Avenue to fix a punctured tire on her Toyota truck one Wednesday afternoon, she sat down at a sidewalk table for a quick salad at nearby Grilly's Restaurant. Wearing black rubber orthopedic boots on his rear paws, Blazer lay quietly at her feet. Joey, leashed to one leg of the table, scanned the area intently. Shortly after Claire settled in to her chair with the meal, Joey, the ace bird hunter, spied a dried sycamore leaf fluttering along the curb. He lunged for it, dumping the table, Claire's salad, her drink, napkin, silverware, and the dressing she prefers "on the side" all over the sidewalk and into the street. This gustatory pandemonium so convulsed an adjacent customer that she apologized to Claire, adding, "I'm sorry. I couldn't help laughing. I could just see it coming when that leaf went by." Claire shrugged it off as one more entry in the liability column of the Brittany Owner's Balance Sheet.

The loss of Max to heavy traffic on East Blithedale Avenue convinced us never to allow the dogs off lead in urban areas except in safe places like our backyard or Dog Bone Park in Novato where they can bust loose and chase each other around. Another venue that lends itself to unfettered romping is the Sierra Nevada mountains where we go cross-country skiing every winter. But one of the frustrations of cross-country skiing at resorts allowing the sport is that dogs are rarely, if ever, welcomed. Though we chafed at the rules, our common sense told us they were right. Loose dogs on prepared ski trails are a formula for disaster: skewered and injured pooches, sprained ankles, and all sorts of other mayhem. Thus we were forced to park the Brittanys in the Jeep until we returned from our tour. To our delight, a sport that originated in Scandinavian countries is catching on in the United States. It is called skijoring, and involves fitting your dog with a specially designed harness and attaching a thick nylon bungee cord to a shock-corded hip belt to buffer his inevitable jerking and lunging. Properly hitched up, you strap on your skis, hold on for dear life, and off you go through the snowy woods. It's a terrific workout for dog and master.

The approaching winter season afforded an opportunity to test Joey's appetite for the winter environment. On a ridge overlooking an enclave of second homes not far from the north shore of Lake Tahoe, Claire and I strapped on our old Norwegian

Epoke cross-country skis. Light and springy, but hopelessly out of date compared with modern fiberglass composites, they required just the right application of grip wax to work right. We each carried a daypack with extra water and snacks, down jacket and wind parka, first aid kit, kicker wax, maps, compass, altimeter, and camera. The lowering pewter-colored sky produced pretty little snow feathers that floated straight down. There was no wind. We laid Blazer on a foam pad in the fiberglass expedition sled Claire had buckled to her hip belt. He was wearing the fiberfill and Gore-Tex parka she had made for Red some years before. She tucked him into the sled's black Cordura gear duffle so just his head was sticking out. His expression reflected the sheer joy of just being out in wild country whether his legs worked or not (which they didn't, or not well enough to propel him through the snow anyway). I was hooked up to Joey, who was prancing around like Sea Biscuit at the Preakness starting line. He was wearing a special skijoring harness with padded chest straps and a hooking point just forward of his tail. A thick elastic cord dangling from a carabiner on my belt was designed to buffer the shock of his exuberant leaps and thrashing about. This was his first time in snow country, so he was clueless about skis, sleds, and skijoring. He would have to trust us and react as best he could to our commands. Soon we were kicking and gliding up the faint trail that leads toward a broad meadow bordered by scattered trees—a monument to severe logging in the 1950s. True to form, Joey threw his shoulders into the harness and forged ahead as if there was a bitch in heat over the next rise. He was pulling so strongly that I rarely had to use my poles. The skis glided soundlessly across the feathery snow. Unfortunately, he developed a fascination for tree wells—those cuplike depressions at the bases of Shasta red firs. We'd be sailing along straight and true when all of a sudden he would veer ninety degrees left or right like a patriot missile, nose vectored on the trunk where some mountain critter had relieved itself. By the time we reached the crest of the ridge, we had developed an understanding of sorts about tree wells and another disruptive habit—circling around behind to wrap me up in the tether. Behind me, Claire was making steady progress, pulling Blazer across a moderate slope, when the sled flipped over. Securely strapped into the cargo duffle, Blazer peered out upside down, calm and composed in the knowledge the situation soon would be corrected. Claire righted the sled, rebuckled her belt, and proceeded. No harm done.

Blurred by the steady snow, the horizon was a monochromatic tableau of distant peaks and ridges. We stopped for a breather. A light wind played with the needles of a young Jeffrey pine nearby. When Joey began to shiver, we placed both dogs side by side in the sled for mutual warmth and broke out water and snacks. Joey got short rations because during the ride up from the Bay Area he had taken the opportunity to wolf down half a bag of chips, six Madeleine cookies, and a whole bag of almonds while I was pumping gas.

As 2003 rolled over into 2004, Blazer's neuropathy continued to weaken his hind legs to the degree that he had to wear his rubber hunting boots on his rear feet even in the house, for better traction on smooth surfaces. Dr. Stan Goldfarb adjusted the spectrum of homeopathic supplements to fortify Blazer's immune system, ease joint pain, and improve his chronic rhinitis. When the occasional digestive disorder or infection sent Blazer into a nosedive, Stan invariably pulled him out of it. Claire became even more doting. "I just love taking care of this little senior," she kept saying. "He's such a gentleman." Cleaning up after incontinence accidents; helping him up the stairs; and maintaining a special diet of ground chicken breast, kibble, sweet potato, and cottage

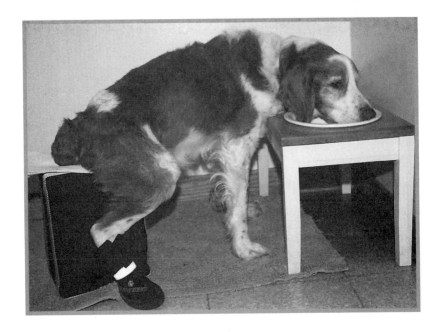

cheese were small prices to pay for having him around. She even devised a square upholstered foam pillow to support his failing hindquarters at mealtime. Now that Blazer was age fifteen and three quarters, his legs had become stiff and brittle, like manzanita twigs. Muscle mass had melted away, leaving his head craggy and his hindquarters wobbly. His weight dropped from thirty-six to twenty-nine pounds. Still, he soldiered on, relishing afternoon adventures through meadows near our house or along the trail by Salt Creek where he savored fragrances of coyote and deer, raccoon and possum, tarweed and lupine.

One Saturday morning in the spring, while I was dressing for a luncheon with U.S. Marine veterans in an East Bay city, Blazer began pacing back and forth through the house, panting heavily, and crying out in a high-pitched, plaintive howl. It was obvious he was in some physical or psychological distress, so I scrubbed the luncheon and drove him and Joey to the Pet Emergency and Specialty Center in San Rafael. While we were waiting for the veterinarian, Blazer paced around the examining room in a circular pattern, as if he had an inner ear problem. He cried out at regular intervals. Dr. Steve Dana examined him and gave him an intravenous sedative that restored his equilibrium somewhat. As we headed out the door, Dr. Dana added the caveat, "This guy is strong willed. We can't find anything seriously wrong with him; but they sometimes crash quickly at this stage of their lives." Was he telling me what I thought he was telling me? Back home, Blazer refused to eat. He rebuffed my attempts to entice him out on a walk by making a U-turn in the middle of the street and heading back home after only a hundred yards. This was not a good sign; in fifteen years he'd never aborted a walk. During all this, Claire was enjoying a well-deserved three-day sojourn to Carmel with her two sisters to celebrate their departed mother's birthday. To avoid ruining her holiday, I refrained from alerting her to Blazer's condition. I did this with some anxiety, knowing how distressed she would be to learn of his condition when she returned. Hoping this was a temporary nosedive, I nursed him along until she arrived home Sunday evening.

Two days later, the quiet intervals between episodes of crying out had shortened. At three o'clock Tuesday morning, Claire and I found ourselves lying on the living room rug cradling the ailing dog, stroking his head and massaging his back for the third time that night. The cries that woke us seemed to rise from deep within his Brittany soul to say, "Help me. I'm trapped in this failing body, but don't want to leave yet." They were the same cries we heard when he became ensnared in vines one afternoon in the backyard, or later when his hindquarters weakened and he couldn't negotiate some obstacle. He yearned to function normally but couldn't. It suddenly hit us that this was not a temporary condition. He was leaving us. We agonized over letting nature's course carry him into a peaceful coma or accelerating the process with euthanasia. The quarter moon threw glowing panels across the walls. Coyotes sang from the near ridge. Finally, Blazer slept. Claire and I dragged ourselves off to bed.

At the breakfast table we made the wrenching decision to end Blazer's suffering and confusion humanely. We both were fighting the temptation to prolong his life for our own selfish indulgence—having him around for one more week, even one more day—against what we knew was best for him. Claire then made the fateful call. Early that afternoon Stan Goldfarb appeared at the door with his assistant Gina. As Blazer lay on his royal blue Double Donut bed in the living room with classical music playing in the background, Gina administered first a sedative and then, ten minutes later, the benevolent potion that released him to wherever it is Brittanys go, especially ones who had touched as many lives as Blazer had. The group fell silent, tearful. As I carried him up the stairs wrapped in his favorite printed Polo

bed sheet to Gina's car, his bony body felt almost bird-like. On the way back inside, the composure I had struggled to maintain so well throughout the procedure dissolved. A bitter brew of fond remembrances, pent-up anxiety, concern for his welfare, and plain old gut-wrenching sorrow burst forth in a cascade of hot tears and uncontrolled sobbing. After a few minutes I regained enough emotional equilibrium to walk outside and tell Stan, "Thanks for everything." He appeared to be struggling almost as much as I was. We shook hands, he mumbled something like "You guys are great," and then they were gone. Angels of mercy.

That evening we pondered how twenty-nine pounds of fur and bones could generate an emotional riptide of such magnitude. "Every morning for almost sixteen years I woke him up and kissed him on the head and told him how much I loved him," Claire said with a quavering voice. "Now I can't do that.

This has been tougher than losing Mom five years ago." It occurred to me that Blazer had been part of my life for a quarter of my sixty-three years. Who would sit beside Joey and me in the truck on the way to Martin Brothers Supply for manure compost or hairy fir bark? The dump lady would have no reason to hand over more than one dog biscuit.

On the April day that Blazer died, we had parked Joey in the backyard, thinking it less complicated and possibly less stressful on a dog who already carried a lot of emotional baggage. Later, someone told us we should have at least let him smell Blazer's body. Perhaps that is the way dogs achieve closure. Who knows? Regardless, we noticed a marked change in Joey from that day on; it was apparent he missed the old guy terribly. He became less inclined to play with his toys. Over the ensuing weeks, his weight dropped from forty-five to thirty-eight pounds, even though we hadn't changed his diet. Our neighbors soon discovered the reason; Joey spent most of the day, rain or shine, running laps in the backyard, beginning soon after Claire drove off to the architect's office at 8:30 in the morning. His circlings traced one small pattern and one larger one, leaving two-inch-deep ruts in the soft soil where the lawn, long dead from the 1976 drought, used to grow. It was as if he was chasing Blazer's spirit; as if, if he ran fast enough, he could catch him and bring him back home again. Alone with squirrels, song birds, and the occasional kite-like shadow of a cruising turkey vulture, Joey succumbed to rising fears that we wouldn't return at the end of the day, or that if we did, there would be angry voices, a gratuitous swat, or a kick in the ribs—the legacy of his abusive former owners. His coursing took him across the graveled pathway under the deck, down the east stairs, across the yard, up the west stairs, hitting the gate with his front paws, then repeating the pattern. Sometimes he looped down into the lower yard past the organic garden and then ran along the west fence to complete the circuit. Soon we discovered he had worn a hole in one of his pads from the constant lapping; he began to favor his left shoulder. When we were home, he ignored his stuffed pheasant toy in favor of solitary naps in the den. His loneliness and grief weighed heavily on us, but what to do?

Six weeks after losing Blazer, Claire was having a difficult day. Even the Sunday chores—laundry; taking care of Pete, the neighbor's cockatiel; shopping; making meals for the coming work week—failed to dilute the festering pain his death continued to inflict on her. "It's been a month and a half, and I feel even worse," she complained while folding towels. "I feel a deep sorrow, an emptiness. Even Mom's death, difficult as it was, didn't hit me this hard." She was beginning to repeat herself. "I keep waking up thinking I heard him cough or his tags jingling. But there's no bed in the corner of the room now. I walk into the living room, see only one day bed, and realize he's gone for good. Sometimes I lie there in the middle of the night wondering if I did the right thing by rescuing Joey. Could Blazer have seen that as a signal it was okay to leave?" She was getting only about four or five hours of sleep a night. Combined with the weight loss and anxiety, she was a wreck. Occasionally, she dozed off at the dinner table right in the middle of a particularly blistering verbal exchange on *The O'Reilly Factor.*

The loss of Blazer had affected each of us in different ways. Claire had her "messy days" when commonplace encounters triggered an emotional reaction: the Hispanic butcher at Whole Foods who asked, "How is the Blazer and the Jose today?" and then walked around the counter to hug her when she stood there speechless, tears streaming down her face; or the lady at Alpha Dog in Mill Valley who asked whether Blazer needed any more of his favorite cookies. About a week after his death, Claire drove up to East San Rafael Veterinary Clinic to pick up his ashes. Bill Estheimer, a veterinarian at the clinic, came over and hugged her when he saw her standing in the reception room holding a polished cedar box the staff had just given her. Stan Goldfarb, the vet who steered Blazer through the shoals of one geriatric crisis after the other with consummate skill, also gave her a hug and added, "Don't worry. He'll come back to you." Prophetic words worth remembering.

Joey, although a diversion and something for Claire to take care of, hadn't yet entered the same chamber of her heart as Blazer. "Just getting through the day reminds me of him," she said over fettuccini Alfredo one evening. "I was a mess on the Tiburon bike path Sunday. Good thing I had on dark glasses when Gordon walked by." Gordon is a retired U.S. Army officer whom Claire befriended after meeting him some years ago on her Sunday walks with Blazer. Like clockwork, Gordon strolls down to Tiburon every Sunday morning to meet his buddies for breakfast at Sweden House. He and Claire compare notes along the way. "Since I had only one dog with me, he asked how I was doing. It was tough for me to get through the explanation about losing Blazer. I miss him so much I would give five years of my life if I could just have him back for one more year or even a few months. For such a little guy he left a huge hole. I'd even do a liver transplant, if that would work for him. In the shower I cry so hard I get dehydrated. Even Joey still feels his energy. He lies on the far end of the sofa in the TV room where I used to pump Blazer's legs every night. He must smell his essence there and on the pillow. I call it the mourning couch. It's funny; he knows not to get up on any other furniture in the house. Just that one. He spends a lot of time on his day bed in the living room. Must smell Blazer there too."

Claire wondered whether Blazer and Joey talked before he died about such things as the responsibility Joey had—to be a good dog and get along with Claire and Bill. She thought some communication must have occurred because Blazer felt he was slipping away and wanted Joey to understand he would be taking his place. She deeply appreciated how I handled Blazer's emergency while she was in Carmel with her sisters. "I will never forget that," she said. "It was above and beyond the call of duty."

A few weeks after Blazer died, Claire bought Joey a huge stuffed monkey. The thing had a goofy bulbous face and a big belly, and weighed about fifteen pounds. We named it Bunky. Claire thought such a tangible furry presence might provide some comfort for Joey. Sure enough, he took a shine to Bunky to the point that he started prancing across the entryway with it in his mouth, looking for all the world like an ant trying to carry a coconut. At the first admonishment from Claire or me, he would scoot back to the den, hoist Bunky up, and drop him back in place on the sofa. Three months after Blazer died, while Claire was reminiscing at the breakfast table, she said the word "Blazer." Joey sat up so abruptly that he bumped his head on the top of his box. His eyes were as big as doorknobs.

On a Sunday in June, we took Joey on a hike to Bon Tempe Lake, one of the nine high lakes that supply water to Marin County residents and businesses. With a quizzical look on his face, he approached the lake cautiously, sneaking up on it as if a pheasant or quail might be hiding in the sedges fringing the shoreline. Little wind waves slapping the mud startled him and he scooted back up the bank toward Claire. Soon his curiosity lured him back down to the water, and he pawed at it and bit it as if it was a living thing. He retrieved floating madrone leaves and dropped them in the grass. It was poignant to watch a four-year-old hunter react so tentatively to the natural world that should have been familiar to him by then. The three and a half years he spent in a small enclosure continued to bedevil him like a psychic straightjacket. We circumnavigated the lake on a dusty trail with Joey forging ahead, then leaping up or down the slope to investigate some sight or smell. The onshore breeze ruffled the cobalt surface of the water and carried the pungent scent of tarweed and the sweet fragrance of new Douglas fir needles. Late afternoon sunrays slicing into deep timber on the south side of the lake brought back memories of summers in the Oregon Cascades as a Forest Service firefighter, trail crew worker, and engineering crewman. On the drive home, we remarked at how simple outings like that expanded Joey's horizons exponentially.

One summer afternoon I left for a river-rafting trip near Rumsey, California, with a group of lawyers, judges, and businessmen. A few hours after I went out the door with all my gear, Joey started a search pattern through the house: in and out of my office, the guest room, the den, our bedroom, the dining room, the kitchen. Claire brought him in from a backyard pee and he started the search pattern all over again while wearing a quizzical expression on his big face. Saturday at 3:00 a.m., Claire heard whining from the kitchen where Joey was supposed to be sleeping in his box. When she opened the door, he raced into the bedroom, vaulted onto the bed, and sat on my side wearing that same quizzical expression. She led him back to the kitchen and tried to salvage what was left of the shredded night. Joey continued the searching through the next day and into Sunday. When I returned from the trip that afternoon, he grabbed his stuffed pheasant toy and went into what Claire calls the Drama King act: whining, muffled crying, and writhing about on the rug as if to say, "I've been too looooonely. Why did you leeeeeve me? I miiiiiiiiised you." The needle on his hug meter had dropped off the scale. This went on for about fifteen minutes until back rubs and head smoothers from his main guy brought him back to normal, whatever that is.

One evening after work I was reviewing e-mail at my computer when I heard Joey bark and snap in the den followed by yelling from Claire, the sound of nails spinning on the parquet floor, and Joey bounding into my office with Claire in hot pursuit, blasting him with a large squirt bottle full of water. Joey scooted past my legs and crashed under the desk. Claire was in a state of high agitation. "Bad dog," she yelled, still taking pot shots with the bottle. "I will not tolerate growling or barking in this house, Buster. Bad dog! You're on the wrong side of me now. Forget about Frosty Paws [Joey's favorite frozen treat]. We're on the outs." More squirting. Joey's soaked head was developing Rastafarian dreadlocks. He was upside down with his big feet in the air. Unconditional craven surrender.

"What the hell happened?" I asked.

"He snapped at me, that's what. I was just shifting him along the sofa to get him back on the sheet when he growled and actually snapped at my face. He may have some baggage, but I'm not going to put up with that. Blazer would never do that." Gone only five months, Blazer still was the gold standard for Brittany behavior. "It's obvious the woman of the house [she meant Joey's former owners] was dark haired and may have mistreated him. But this is going to stop."

"Did he bite you?"

"No, but he was close. That's never happened before, and it's going to stop. I'm willing to try to get him past his baggage, but this is unacceptable."

She turned and stalked out of my office. Joey stared up at me as if Governor Schwarzenegger had just called the warden at San Quentin with a last minute reprieve of his death sentence. He put his big wet head in my lap and groaned.

In midsummer, Fun Day at the Northern California Brittany

Club at Hastings Island in Solano County gave us the first chance to test Joey's talents as a field dog. Whiskey, an eleven-year-old Irish setter, was Joey's mate for the sixth brace. While we were waiting for the dogs and handlers ahead of us to clear the field, we stood talking with some members of the club beneath an alder tree. The day was warming up and the shade felt good. Earlier, Joey had wandered out on the levee, grabbed a chukar in his mouth—a chukar that had been shot earlier in the day and was lying on the levee—and fetched it dutifully to me, just like a trained hunter. Another layer peels off, I thought to myself. Astonished, I chucked the chukar into the field. Joey bounded after it and brought it back to me, repeating the feat two more times in a row. Things were looking up for next season. The occasional crack of shotguns a hundred yards away caught his attention, but didn't seem to spook him. While we chatted with our new-found friends about dogs, travel, dogs, the price of gas, dogs, and the coming election, Terry, a volunteer bird planter and owner of Will, an energetic three-month-old Brittany pup, brought a live chukar out of the holding box at his feet. Before he could let Will see and smell what the pup would be looking for in the field, the bird fluttered his wings and Will scooted for cover behind Terry's wife, Dainese. After a few more unsuccessful attempts to lure Will out from behind Dainese, Terry passed the bird in front of Joey, whose big amber eyes were locked on it. Before Terry could react, he was holding a headless chukar. Faster than the eye could follow, Joey had lunged forward and decapitated it cleanly, dropping the head on the ground. Claire, who had been holding Joey from behind, grabbed him like an alligator wrestler and pried open his mouth, thinking he had swallowed the head and would choke on it. Later, she said she was ready to throw a Heimlich maneuver on him. The assembled group sat stunned for a few moments, then burst into excited babble about the lightening speed and unexpected ferocity of the spectacle. "After all," one of the wives—an attractive brunette— said with a forgiving tone in her voice, "it's their natural prey." I offered that he probably had watched one too many Al Qaeda beheading videos. The group pretty much took it in stride once the initial shock and awe wore off. The judges called our brace, and we released the dogs. Joey took off into the field and ran around and around, bolting between the hummocks, racing across the dry grasses, scattering terrified chukars to the four winds. Not once did he freeze into a point. So much for next season.

On our way to the Jeep for the ride home to Mill Valley, one of the members convinced us to watch the conformation session that was forming up at the picnic area. She said it was very informal and an enjoyable way to determine whether your dog has any conformation or show-ring potential. Why not, we thought. Brittanys are supposed to be capable in field and ring. We preferred the field to the choreographed precision of the show ring, but what would the downside to the conformation session be? Claire tried unsuccessfully to convince me to lead Joey into the ring. Knowing his clownish nature, I declined. After all, I was the field handler, remember? It was now her turn.

Joey performed adequately during the prancing and running around part of the conformation exercise. When it came time for the handlers to "stack" their dogs so the judge could make certain they had all their body parts, Joey leapt into the air, did a half gainer, and fell on his back writhing and squirming around in a "grass bath" as Claire termed it. The gallery joined the judge in a burst of laughter. But it was not all wasted effort and time. After the hilarity died down and order was restored, the judge handed out ribbons, including one to Joey. It was his first ribbon—a shiny purple one emblazoned "PARTICIPANT"—and was duly preserved in his scrapbook. So much for the show ring.

October storms sailing over Mount Tamalpais pounded our narrow valley with torrential downpours, turning the backyard into a quagmire. When I met Joey at the gate after work on those

days, he looked more like a Weimaraner than a Brittany—covered
with grey mud from head to foot after running laps all day. It
took twenty minutes to shower him down and get him ready for
the evening walk through the neighborhood. In the shower, his
coat flattened out to reveal that his muscular haunches and deep
chest were even more pronounced than they used to be. Lanky
to begin with, he was developing the physique of a marathoner.

We could only speculate what sort of baggage triggered
his lapping behavior. Perhaps neural scars from being kept in a
small enclosure in his former owner's backyard for three years, a
confusing trip to the pound, the pandemonium, the stench of
fear and anxiety and death, the ear-shredding cacophony of caged
dogs, the uncertainty of removal to David's foster home in Mill
Valley, then our arrival, the new environment, and the sudden loss
of old man Blazer—all these may have conspired to unnerve
him. Each day he probably wondered whether we would return
or whether different people would come to take him away to
another place. Stuffed toys remained forlorn in his wicker basket;
the pheasant, sock monkey, quail, nutcracker soldier, fuzzy pretzel,
road-kill crab, soccer ball, moo cow, weasel, and yellow duck hadn't
had a good workout since Blazer died. Joey's customary burst of
energy after breakfast had given way to naps on the den sofa—
the only piece of furniture he was allowed to enjoy since we
found him curled up on it the day after Blazer died. Joey evi-
dently had noticed the leg therapy sessions Claire administered
faithfully to Blazer for ten minutes every night during the news

and assumed it was okay for Brittanys to bunk in there. Even an attempt to interest him in a game of toss the road-kill crab failed to elicit much more than a half-hearted response.

Shortly after Joey's one-year anniversary at our house, I was trying to accomplish some task on the computer in my office when a Microsoft error message popped up on the screen. "Damn," I muttered softly under my breath. In the blink of an eye, Joey scooted in from his bunk in the den and was at my side looking up with those huge amber eyes asking, "What did I do wrong?" A week later I was trying to pay the bills and balance our checkbook when I came cross another one of Claire's indecipherable register entries. "Dammit," I said, sending Joey into a paroxysm of whining and fervent tail wagging while pushing a stuffed hedgehog wearing a Santa hat in my face. Then he threw up all over the stuffed toy. Three years of abuse at the hands of his former owners kept reverberating.

Regardless, the Brittany Owner's Manual cites the duty and responsibility to keep your Brittany challenged and entertained, especially during morale slumps; so some sort of outing seemed in order. Almost a year to the day after Joey found himself pulling me across a frozen meadow near Donner Pass, we gave him another shot at skijoring. Bear Valley, about a four-hour drive east of our home, sits at the 7000-foot elevation in the Sierra Nevada range along historic Highway 4 just west of Ebbetts Pass. We tooled on up there in our Jeep one Friday afternoon and settled into Base Camp Lodge, a rustic cedar-shingled bed-and-breakfast run by Aaron and Kimi Johnson, a young couple who also provide mountain guide services under the banner "Mountain Adventure Seminars." Rob, their chef, whips up surprisingly sophisticated concoctions for dinner—mostly from his own ingenuity and instinct—that belie the isolated nature of the place. His menu, including grilled rack of lamb, portobello mushroom piccata, and spinach manicotti, would give any fine restaurant in the Bay Area a hard run for its money. The small but comfortably furnished rooms are reasonably priced and complement the ground floor where game rooms, fireplace, library, dining area, and bar beckon families as well as singles. Until the Johnsons acquired it a few years ago, it was called the Red Dog Lodge and enjoyed a reputation as a place where CalTrans snowplow and highway construction crews, highway patrol officers, truckers, loggers, fishermen, hangers on, and assorted ski bums could congregate and raise hell. Evidence of their gustatory and alcoholic excesses still can be found in the form of carved signatures and bon mots sealed under a layer of epoxy on the top of the sawed plank bar. Under the Johnson's stewardship, the lodge lives up to its name as a family-friendly base of operations for cross-country skiers and mountaineers of every stripe.

By mid morning of the next day, Claire, Joey, and I were chugging up a broad snowy ridgeline east of Bear Valley. I was carrying a daypack with lunch, water, medical gear, survival kit, extra clothing, lightweight snow shovel, and avalanche beacon. Claire had strapped on her K2 telemark skis fitted with kicker skins for the thousand-foot climb. The plan was to ski to the top of the ridge, have lunch, strip off the skins, and then enjoy the ride back down. It would be a full day. Joey, wearing his padded skijoring harness, charged upward against the elastic bungee cord, huffing steam into the sun-washed morning air. Soon we could see south to the volcanic monoliths of the Dardanelles and the peaks of the Emigrant Wilderness beyond. Even though it was January, the stable weather and the exertion allowed us to travel comfortably in long-sleeve polypropylene shirts. Throwing his shoulders into the harness, Joey pulled me along the flat sections with only light poling on my part. He was getting one hell of a workout. Just short of the ridge top, we dug a lunch bivouac, complete with seats and a nest for Joey to curl up in. The winter sun flowed across the slope like warm honey.

Lengthening shadows prompted us to strip the skins off our skis, tighten our boots, and prepare for the enjoyable part of the sojourn—dropping a thousand feet down to the trailhead. I would just as soon be hooked to a runaway boulder as be tied to Joey on the descent, so I let him romp along beside me off lead until he veered off into a tree well after a Douglas squirrel and Claire yelled, "Get him back on the leash! Didn't you learn anything from Max?" Her distrust of off-lead Brittanys was not misplaced, so we compromised by leapfrogging the dog between one-hundred-yard descents. Claire took off a hundred yards down the slope, stopped, and called Joey. I released him and he churned downhill dragging his bungee at full speed, spraying snow everywhere. Claire snagged him so I could ski downhill past her to repeat the process. It worked like a charm; Joey got to gallop flat out, leaving us to fine-tune our telemark turns.

A month later, Dr. Larry Friedman called me at my office in San Francisco and invited me to join him on Friday at Black Point Sports Club. "If you still have that Brittany, bring him along, and he can watch Cookie do her stuff," he suggested. "It will be a good training session." Now fully retired, Larry had been our personal physician for many years. Claire likes to recount the many times he reeled off open-ended stories about his beloved black Labrador Waldo while palpating her abdomen for anomalies during the annual physical at his office in Greenbrae. Sadly,

Waldo's aging bladder and other infirmities eventually led to his demise, leaving Friedman dogless for a while. His new dog, Cookie, was an elegant three-year-old German wirehaired pointer. Professionally trained, she was well on her way to the title of master hunter.

When I met Larry at the sports club on Friday morning, the back side of a Pacific storm blocked the sun. Dark-bottomed cumuli floating slowly northeast trailed veils of rain across the distant hills. The weatherman predicted clearing, so Larry and I unloaded our gear beside a field that had been reserved earlier that morning but was open to all comers after ten o'clock. Larry had been at the upland hunting game long enough to have top-notch stuff: a Browning Citori 16-gauge shotgun, top of the line vest, and Bean's hunting boots. Cookie wore an electronic collar. The tall, fit, sixtyish hunter and the trim German wirehaired pointer made a fetching pair against the dun-colored backdrop of the field. By contrast, Joey wore one of Blazer's old red collars and trailed a twenty-foot nylon training lead. Earlier, I had boasted to Larry that Joey had learned the recall command very well on our afternoon walks in the hills. "He's a hundred percent on the recall," I bragged. "Whether it's the 'come' command or a long blast on this whistle, he scoots over to my left side and sits. Then I give him a treat. Works every time." By then Larry had popped the leash off Cookie, and she was exploring hummocks and tuffs of grass likely to conceal birds. She was methodical, thorough, and responsive to Larry's occasional commands—a pleasure to watch. At Larry's urging, I released Joey's twenty-foot nylon training lead. He charged at top speed around us in ever expanding orbits, leaping over hummocks and bushes, and tearing across open ground. Soon he was twenty yards out, then forty. At fifty yards of this nonsense, I called out, "Joey, come!" No response. A long blast on the whistle. No response. More frantic long blasts produced the same result. He was out of control. Two hunters wearing orange caps were working the levee to the north and west of us. At a hundred and fifty yards I lost sight of Joey. Then a speck of white appeared, stopped, froze. Joey was on point. Ten seconds later, a cock pheasant exploded out of the grass in a blur of wings and bored its way south toward the slate-colored bay. It would have been a tough shot, even with a regulation Remington sniper rifle with a Redfield scope. Ten minutes later, the white dot reappeared, stopped, froze: another point followed by a feathery trajectory fading into the now brightening disc of the sun.

"Sir, are you hunting, or just training your dog?" asked a lean young man who had just parked his pickup truck along the access road and walked into the field. I assumed he was with the Black Point staff. "Neither," I responded. "I've been trying to get this dog under control for twenty minutes."

"Well, sir, I'm going to have to ask you to take him out of the field. He's bustin' all the birds, and it's not fair to the other hunters." He walked back to his truck and took off toward the office buildings in the distance.

Embarrassed, I yelled louder and blew the whistle longer. Joey's orbits began to contract. He swung in closer and closer until he was streaking past ten feet from me, trailing the soggy training lead. I sprinted through the grass and stomped on the end of the lead, throwing Joey into a back flip. He landed belly up, feet in the air with a mischievous look on his face that radiated "I knew what I was doing every minute. I am so smart; I knew you couldn't catch me. It was fabulous fun, and I will do it again if I get the chance." He'd used up his chances, at least for that day.

Brady

Ecstatic romping in bird fields notwithstanding, Joey's lapping in the backyard continued unabated. His loneliness weighed heavily on us, but what to do? Finally Claire's infallible instinct and intuition kicked in. She started surfing the American Brittany Rescue Web site for a likely candidate as a companion for Joey. She also inquired about a new litter in Empire, a town on the Tuolumne River southeast of Modesto, California. The breeder, an engaging, avuncular sort who referred to his dogs as "my kids," told her over the phone that the pups were distantly related to Blazer through the Lost River line. This further fueled her notions of spiritual resurrection. I wasn't buying it, even when she showed me photographs the breeder sent her. "They're cute," I responded. "But all Brittany pups are cute as the devil and none of these calls out to me. I think Brady, the little guy you saw on the ABR Web site, looks a lot like Blazer. Check out those eyes. There's something about them. Besides, he's at a foster home in San Jose.

Why don't we drive down Friday and look him over? We can take Joey to see if they hit it off."

Sandy, the woman who was fostering Brady, greeted us at her house in San Jose and motioned us over to the side yard. Claire looked down at the diminutive Brittany peering through the wrought-iron gate next to her feet and said softly, "My God. Blazer is back. Look at that face. He looks just like Blazer." Sandy was generous with her time, letting us sit on the sidelines while Brady and Joey raced around the backyard lawn, fetched sticks and bones, and terrorized the five hens and a rooster in a chicken coop. Maggie, Sandy's six-year-old liver-colored Brittany, ambled over and greeted us with obligatory tail wagging, then drifted back inside. Sandy explained that from the beginning, Maggie wanted nothing to do with Brady's antics, especially his habit of chasing his stump of a tail, and tossing toys in the air and catching them. Maggie even growled at him a couple of times when he got too feisty around her. During a quick sidebar conference, I assured Claire that I was on board about adopting Brady on the spot. Sandy helped Claire fill out the papers, we handed over a fat contribution to ABR, and off we went up the road with a brace of Brittanys.

We pulled up in our driveway in Mill Valley late that afternoon, and Brady leaped out of the Jeep. He had been such a blur at his foster home, I hadn't taken time to look him over in detail. For a nine month old, he looked compact and undersized. Compared to Joey's big fan feet, Brady's looked almost rabbit-like, with tiny toes; his leg bones looked delicate. Each paw had a dark mahogany patch, making it appear muddy at first glance. He appeared longer than he was high, a variation from the standard square dimensions of a show-quality Brittany. His coat was the standard patchwork of ivory and cinnamon, the cinnamon parts being darker and richer than Joey's. Closer inspection revealed his coat was parted the length of his spine like Alfalfa's hair in the 1930s movie series *Spanky and Our Gang*. From his haunches, an unruly three-inch-high ruffle of feather-like fur sprouted up and curled forward in an epic cowlick, making him appear hunch-backed from the side. Could there have been a bantam rooster in the woodpile? Everything about him was tiny, much to Claire's delight because he resembled Blazer and he was easier to carry than Joey, the forty-nine-pound load. From then on I referred to

Brady as the miniature Brittany. We speculated about how he and his sibling wound up on Olive Highway in Oroville; perhaps the owner's bitch whelped a litter of pups and Brady and his sibling didn't measure up to marketing or hunting standards in appearance or performance. Not being able to bring himself to drop them into the lake in a weighted burlap bag, the owner may have abandoned them to their fate on the road. Fortunately, Brady survived. Unfortunately, his sibling did not.

Bonnie Trammell, manager of the Northwest SPCA shelter in Oroville, California, explained what role her facility played in Brady's transition from abandoned stray to privileged companion.

"Brady came in January 28, 2005. Somebody brought him in to the shelter. He was found on Olive Highway near the Gold Country Casino. He had no collar. His brother had been struck by a vehicle and was lying severely injured on the shoulder of the road. He died later at the shelter. We put Brady in a kennel for dogs that just came in and aren't available for adoption yet. After we've held them for the mandatory four business days, they're eligible for adoption.

"My gut feeling is somebody dumped Brady and his brother, just dumped them out of the car. Hunters are a different breed of people. I do believe that. I actually know people like that. Some of them dump them on the road, or leave them in the field if they don't hunt. Dumping them somewhere because they won't hunt goes over the line for me, because we would gladly place them. Some hunters, though, who are responsible hunters—whose dogs are their companions—do take care of them. We've had dogs here in this shelter that have tracking collars on and the hunter tracks them right to the shelter and picks them up."

Bonnie pulls out all the stops to place abandoned animals. She uses Pet Finders, rescue organizations, newspapers, anything she can do to get them adopted. "We got Brady in the ABR system by just calling them up," she told me. "Brady was not here very long. He arrived on January 28. Nobody called or came by for him, so he left to a foster home on February 7." I thanked Bonnie for rescuing little Brady and wrote out a nice contribution to the shelter.

This was the second time in two years we had called on American Brittany Rescue, the first being when we adopted Joey in the fall of 2003. There is no doubt in my mind that the organization's high professional standards and efficiency, as well as our positive experience with Joey despite his "baggage" and behavioral quirks, prompted us to knock on their door again when Joey appeared to need a companion after Blazer died. The ABR Web site declares in part, "American Brittany Rescue was formed in 1991 as a cooperative effort of Brittany owners, breeders, trialers, and fanciers who believe we have a responsibility not only for our own dogs and the dogs we produce, but for our breed as a whole. Because many rescue dogs can be traced one to three generations back to a recognized breeder, we believe all breeders should take it upon themselves to assist Brittanys in need in any way they can. The purpose of rescue is to take in stray, abandoned, surrendered and/or impounded purebred Brittanys, provide them with foster care, health and temperament screening, offer an opportunity for rehabilitation if necessary, assure their health, and place them in new homes. Brittanys can make wonderful family dogs and excel in many areas, but they are not for everyone. They are active, playful, energetic dogs who require personal attention every day. If you'd like to learn whether a Brittany is a good choice for you, your family and/or your lifestyle, please read *Choosing a Brittany*. Although many rescued dogs do hunt with their new families, our primary concern is finding homes where they will be a valued member of the family."

Six weeks into Brady's adoption, Claire is still buzzing about it. "Forget about the one-carat diamond earrings, ha, ha, ha, for our anniversary or my birthday or Christmas or whatever," she told me after dinner one night. She was finishing up the dishes and steam from the sink had frosted the reading glasses that make her eyes appear larger than they really are. "Brady is all that rolled into one. He's just precious. I love him so much. He is exactly what I've needed since we lost Blazer. He has brightened my life. When Blazer died I was in Brittany hell. Now I'm in heaven. Don't get me wrong. Joey is a great dog, and we're lucky to have him. It's just that he's partial to you. He's a big old needy 'Yup,

Yup' Brittany who's always looking for reassurance and validation. He's not a snuggler like Brady is. I'll be folding laundry in
the utility room and he'll wander in and just snuggle up into my
lap, making those little squeaky hamster grunts and kissing my
chin. And he's smart. Look how quickly he picked up 'sit,' 'down,'
and 'come.' It took just under a week for him to learn about peeing in the house. He's so cool. He's even as gassy as Blazer was."

She's glad I steered her away from the litter in Empire,
nice as the breeder seemed, and as connected to Blazer's bloodline as the pups were, and over to Brady at the San Jose foster
home. "It's eerie how much Brady resembles Blazer, not just
physically," she told me. "He even crosses his paws like Blazer did.
And his left eye is a little walleyed. Yesterday I found about twenty
feet of toilet paper reeled off the downstairs roll. Blazer definitely
is back. He even raided your office trash basket the other day, and
got a package of my cupcake papers out of the pantry. Whenever
Brady gets into something he shouldn't, Joey comes running
over, eyes as big as golf balls, wagging his tail furiously as if to say,
'He's into something again and it wasn't me.' Like the time he
emptied my cookbooks off the shelf and then overturned the
basket of 'cheater' reading glasses. Joey was a mess."

The notion that Blazer's spirit may have sparked over to
Brady kept bugging Claire. After all, she tried to convince me,
the timing was right. Blazer had died about ten months before,
close to the time Brady would have been whelped. Even though
I'm a hard science, nuts-and-bolts type of guy, she repeatedly

tried to sell me on this metaphysical hoo-ha. Even though she was right about the physical resemblance—crossed paws when he's lying down, slightly wall-eyed gaze, deliberate and measured approach to eating, wastebasket raids, flatulence, and his gentle-manly demeanor—she failed to make a convincing case that it's anything more than a coincidence.

Although I was not yet ready to embrace the Shirley MacLaine philosophy of soul transference, even I began to notice uncanny similarities to Blazer. For instance, just as Blazer did, Brady detoured around the three higher steps at the top of the side-yard stairs—the ones Claire continues to berate me for miscalculating when building them ten years ago; he's a ferocious digger—my carefully tamped, decomposed granite walkways around the vegetable garden now resemble the neighborhood surrounding the Green Zone compound in Baghdad—mortar craters everywhere. Like Blazer, he enjoys gnawing on things. The Direct TV cable in the basement looks like black chewing gum after the fact. The shingle I use as a pooper-scooper is splin-tered and holey. My autographed copy of Kevin Starr's *Coast of Dreams* has lost its dust jacket and is missing half the front cover. The wicker toy basket is frayed. The toilet paper roll in the guest bathroom looks like someone shot it with number six birdshot. A tiny tooth jammed the mute button on the TV remote into the underlying circuitry, rendering the device worthless for watching anything but the Shopping Channel. Life is back to normal.

The remarkable synergy between Brady and Joey seemed

to have returned a measure of equilibrium and pumped a sense of youthful vitality into the household. Seeing Joey roughhouse with Brady or chase him pell-mell down the hallway or lick the sleep out of his eyes in the morning was a welcomed change from his endless laps of separation anxiety and frustration in the backyard. One morning before leaving for work, I watched with considerable apprehension as Brady padded over to Joey, who was gnawing on a large bone in the living room. He lay down next to Joey and slowly took the bone in his mouth. Joey gave it up and began to lick the inside of Brady's inflamed ear. I went out the door reassured that Brady had found not only a new home but a new brother.

Brady's new home also harbored a plethora of strange sights, smells, and sounds that set off his squeaky puppy bark at regular intervals: someone walking by on the road; a nearby dog cutting up; June Cooperman's kids bouncing on the trampoline next door, a door slamming. PetSafe came to the rescue once again; on the days Claire drove off to manage the architectural office in Sausalito, she fitted Brady with a red nylon collar containing a small plastic box with two $3/8$-inch-long probes that rested against the skin of his throat. Vibration from Brady's barking triggers a mild electronic shock (much like static electricity). Within a few days, only the most irresistible stimulant set Brady off. Even then it was short lived: modern technology at its best.

Brady's unbridled fascination with anything airborne and Joey's ballistic approach to the field prompted me to explore ways to evaluate their potential as hunters. On a Sunday morning in June, Claire and I met a trainer, Joe Langlois, by pre-arrangement at the property of Grab and Grow, a landscaping and construction material outfit outside the town of Sebastopol in Sonoma County. The dirt road off the main drag led us past miniature mountains of landscaping and gardening material, then to a cluster of ramshackle outbuildings and barns and two small houses where several Hispanic children were playing in the front yard.

A dry north wind sweeping down the coast from Oregon buffeted the high branches of oak and sycamore trees and sent ripples across grasses rising in rich green oases across a newly mown field that would serve as a proving ground to determine whether Joey and Brady had the right stuff for bird hunting. Seven turkey vultures and one red-tailed hawk floated over the pasture, drawn by a rich mélange of baby rabbits, ducklings, and field mice the mower had left scattered in its path two days before.

Joe was stocky and about 46 years old, with square features and a full head of rich brown hair streaked with grey. He wore a well-stained bird-hunting vest, jeans, and boots. A fireman at the Ross Valley firehouse, he lives in the nearby community of Penngrove and trains bird dogs in his spare time. The owner of Grab and Grow lets him use the field as a training ground. Although aficionados of bird-dog superstars might not know it because handlers get all the notoriety, Joe had trained three national champions in this modest field.

On the drive up to Sebastopol, Claire admitted she was very nervous about letting Brady run around off lead. After only three months, he had wormed his way into that special chamber of her heart like Blazer. A sure sign of the strength of this bond are her extra names for him: Brady O'Brady, Sweet-A-Pea, My Little Man, Little Prince without the Crown, the Bradester. "What if he gets through the fence and runs away?" she pondered. "He hasn't been off lead since we got him, except at Black Point Beach in Sea Ranch, which is surrounded by bluffs. I don't think I could take it if we lost him." I suggested that we check out the area when we got there, and then she and she alone could make the decision whether to continue with the session.

As I unloaded the gear from the truck, Claire huddled

with Joe about her fear of losing Brady and whether field training would dull his affectionate qualities. "Bird dogs can be good
home companions and still be great in the field," he assured her.
"They can do both. Living inside doesn't ruin a bird dog and
vice versa. That's just a myth. As for them getting away, we just
don't lose dogs out here." As we walked over to the field, Joe pat-
ted her on the shoulder and said, "It's okay, Mom. He'll do fine."

In a low-key voice, Joe explained that he had planted
three chukars in the field and that now he would observe each
dog's movements and reaction to the birds.

Joey went first, racing out across the browning field trailing a twenty-foot nylon training lead. We were prepared for the
Patriot Missile act that blasted him over the horizon beyond gun
range as he did at Black Point Sports Club the previous winter
and at the Fun Day with the Northern California Brittany Club
during the summer. To our surprise, he circled back a few times,
trotted over to check out likely hiding places in the remnant
grass, and locked into a solid point five feet from the burlap bag
containing Joe's chukars. "Look. He's pointing the bag," said Joe.
"That means he's probably never been worked in the field. Most
dogs when they're five years old know enough not to point a bag
of birds. They even ignore songbirds."

When Joey sniffed around in earnest beyond the bag, a
chukar exploded straight up and drilled itself through the wind-
scoured sky. Joey raced along behind until it disappeared. The
next bird spooked him. Joey locked on with a staunch point,

then backed off and dropped his ears when Joe began to kick the grass. The bird went up, threaded itself through the overarching branches, and flew out of sight. Joe noted Joey's reaction with keen interest. "Look at that. He was a little spooked by the bird," he said. "He might have had some training after all, and somebody overdid the electronic collar. Shocked him to get him to 'whoa' near the bird so he wouldn't bust it. Now Joey associates birds with a collar that bites him in the neck. We'll be able to help him get beyond that this summer. A lot of hunters and some trainers push the training pace too fast."

Joe prefers a measured, results-oriented pace combined with limited use of electronic toys, using the electronic collar only as a last resort. That way, he claims, the training has more staying power. Joe finds the girls harder to train than the boys, meaning that females mature faster, but aren't as consistent and focused as the males eventually turn out to be. He much prefers to train males, who tend to stay on track after the training sessions end. Interestingly, the German wirehaired pointer in the crate in the back of his truck was a pretty female. I was beginning to like this guy.

Little Brady was next. He jackrabbited out into the sun-drenched, windswept field with wild abandon, darting after grasshoppers and butterflies, and the occasional songbird. Joe speculated that Brady was younger than the twelve months we had calculated based on information we got from the Oroville shelter. "He has little puppy feet and he hunts more like a puppy, using his eyes instead of his nose," he said. "I think he's more like eight or nine months." Brady darted around a copse of high grass and grabbed a chukar just as it sprang into the air. Joe let him play with it for about five minutes, and then we moved to another area of the field. Hunting only with his eyes, Brady didn't detect the bird Joe had planted in the grass at our feet. When Joe kicked him up, the bird took off, gaining speed over the field with Brady racing along underneath, emitting little puppy yelps of joy and excitement. To Claire's consternation, they both headed straight for a rusty fence bordering the field. In a flash, the bird was beyond it and Brady somehow was through it, trailing the green lead behind him. Then the bird banked to the right and sailed back over the field. Brady threaded himself right back through the fence and continued the chase until it was obvious the bird was gone for good. Claire sighed a heavy sigh of relief when Brady rejoined the group. Joe then moved over to another island of tall grass beneath an oak tree. "Look how he's hunting with his eyes," he said. "He's right next to a bird, but hasn't noticed it yet." Brady scanned the field and the horizon beyond for grasshoppers and butterflies and other flying things. Distracted momentarily by our further discussion of hunting traits, we looked back down to see Brady locked into an awkward point with his nose inches from the grass and his body bent like a fortune cookie. "That's what we're looking for," said Joe. "Now he's hunting with his nose."

Back at the truck, Joe was upbeat about the potential of

both dogs. "If you just want a hunting dog, we should be able to do enough sessions this summer to be ready for the season." Presumably he meant we wouldn't be vying for national field trial champion status, but we would have two dogs who knew hunting basics. Claire raised her eyebrows when he said, "Brady's got more pizzazz than Joey. And he's younger. He's going to be easier to handle. Joey's a little headstrong, but I think we can overcome that. Also, he's five years old. Usually, I don't take older, headstrong dogs. But I think Joey will come along with a little work." Unlike some viszlas and shorthairs, Brittanys are "softer," according to Joe. "You hit a viszla or a shorthair in the head with a two by four and they'll do anything for you from then on. Brittanys, they're softer. They'll pout for a while, but then they always come back on track and get down to business. I'd like to think these guys could be hunting as a brace by the end of summer. You know, one honoring the other's point when they come upon a bird."

When I mentioned Joey's exaggerated concept of the proper distance separating dog from hunter in the field, Joe responded, "It's okay for him to be out that far as long as he holds the point." I was a little skeptical. I thought perhaps I still should invest in a Remington sniper rifle with a Redfield scope.

Oddly, our planned sessions with Joe never materialized. For whatever reason—schedule overload, second thoughts about a hardheaded Brittany, or something else—Langlois never returned the many voice-mail messages I left on his phone.

July rolled into August, cool and foggy along the coast and sunny but breezy inland. Early one Saturday morning I tried one last time to convince Claire to take Brady along with Joey and me to the Fun Day at the Northern California Brittany Club at Hastings Island, but she wanted nothing to do with it. "He's only been with us six months, and you've seen how he is at Dog Bone Park. We yell and blow the whistle, and he keeps tearing across the grass after the chimney swifts. It's like we're not even there. I love him so much I just don't want to take the chance of losing him. Maybe when he's trained on the recall better."

By the time Joey and I pulled into the parking lot at the Hastings Island Hunting Club west of Rio Vista, most of the dogs and owners had registered with the club secretary and were waiting for the puppy braces to finish gamboling about in an adjacent field. Joey was scheduled for the seventh intermediate brace, which they would call in about an hour and a half: just enough time to implement the plan I conceived after his embarrassing performances last year. After watching him bounce around the fields at top speed like a ricocheting pinball, it occurred to me he just needed to burn off some energy before the formal event. We strolled down the road to a field that was partly flooded and had a decent amount of cover. There, I tried to apply the lessons I learned in the book *Qualify: A Guide to Successful Handling in AKC Pointing Breed Tests* by Mark Powell: move swiftly down wind, then bring the dog back upwind deliberately, encouraging him to explore likely hiding places. That way, he's more likely to catch the cone of bird scent drifting toward him on the breeze. To my surprise, Joey moved out into the field, then ranged carefully back and forth about twenty yards in front of me, checking out hummocks and bushes at a measured pace. Even after I released the long training lead, he stayed relatively close, responding to my short blasts on the whistle for direction changes. It was as if he was a different dog: none of the ballistic madness, tearing about through the field, scattering terrified chukars to the four winds, ignoring my whistle and hoarse yelling. After forty-five minutes, we headed back to the clubhouse. On the way, Joey dropped down for a quick rest under a tree. Theory affirmed.

After a half hour, "Bill Buchanan with Joey for the intermediate brace" boomed over the loudspeaker. Off we went to a field across the road. Next to the levee stood the judge near a hunter in his late sixties with a young female Brittany. "As soon as you reach the first flag," explained the judge, pointing one hundred yards north to a DayGlo banner on a pole, "do a left turn. Then go to the next flag and take a left. Then you're in the bird field. Good luck, gentlemen. You may cast your dogs."

The Brittany on our right took off like a cannonball on a parabolic trajectory toward the horizon. Joey hadn't gone ten yards before her owner started yelling and blowing a whistle like a drunken referee. Joey's rescue baggage kicked in: he lowered his head and fell back to my side, almost cowering. "Find the birds, Joey. Birds! Let's go!" I encouraged him while points evaporated in the judges' mental ledgers. The garrulous racket to our right was getting on my nerves now. Why didn't the judge admonish him for what they call hacking—excessive commands and noise? Then the man's Brittany tore off down the levee out of sight to our left. The owner quit yelling. Thank God. Joey recovered and started working the field tentatively, then more boldly. Still somewhat spooked, he was not up to speed. Psychological scars left by three years of verbal and perhaps physical abuse at the hands of his former owners had not completely healed. We made the turn upwind into the bird field. Loudmouth's Brittany had returned by then and locked on point. Her owner fired a blank. Match point. We moved a short distance and ran out of field. A judge standing on the levee road before us generously directed me to take him around again. We moved quickly downwind, then turned back into the bird field. After twenty yards, Joey pointed a hummock of grass. "Whoa. Whoa," I commanded. Seconds later, a chukar exploded into the air and drilled itself out of sight to the north with Joey bounding along behind, ignoring my "whoa" command and blasts from the whistle: back to the old ballistic mode. I shook my head and left the field so the next brace could get going. Joey joined me at the levee, wearing that same expression of utter rapture and intentional irresponsibility I had seen in February: like a joyriding teenager pulled over by the cops. Back to the drawing board.

Still convinced Joey had potential, I arranged to meet Mike Sutsos, a renowned trainer of pointing dogs and the owner of Black Point Sports Club, a month later for an hour session to further assess Joey's potential. On a Monday in August precisely at 10:25 a.m., I rolled up to a group of buildings shaded by eucalyptus and oak trees. To the south, a checkerboard of mowed fields fanned out all the way to San Francisco Bay. In the shade, the fog-born breeze was bordering on chilly. I was a few minutes early for my appointment, so I entered the club and found it, as expected, cluttered with hunting memorabilia: a stuffed deer head, stuffed pheasants, quails, and chukars. The walls were adorned with paintings and photographs of hunting scenes. A sofa faced the fireplace. Off the main entrance, a door led into a small office. An old female Labrador with pendulous dugs tapped a welcome on the wall with her tail. There was no one else around.

After twenty minutes, I began to wonder whether there had been some miscommunication with Mike Sutsos, who was supposed to meet me at 10:30 a.m. As a San Francisco business-man, I have punctuality imbedded in my DNA. I told myself to relax; the billing clock was not ticking. Revenues wouldn't be affected. The only expenditure to that point had been gas and time. Outside, a truck ground to a halt. It was a 1960s vintage Jeep J10 flatbed fitted with a jury-rigged platform for bird cages over the front bumper and three wire kennels on the bed snugged up against the back of the cab. Yellow nylon ropes hung off the sides. A five-gallon jug of water was strapped in near the cab. It looked like something out of a Road Warrior movie.

A large man in his forties, wearing a hunting vest, shorts, and hunting boots stepped out and introduced himself as Mike. We exchanged pleasantries and soon were bumping along a dirt road in the vintage truck headed for one of the fields, with Joey stuffed into a wire crate on the flatbed. On the way, I described Joey's uneven evolution as a bird dog. Mike outlined a rudimen-tary assessment regimen: he would plant several pigeons in the grass, observe how Joey reacted, then go from there. I brought Joey out of the wire crate on the bed of the truck, then Mike fitted him with a DogTra electronic collar. Pushing my fingers beneath the collar, I said, "Jeez, Mike. That's pretty tight. Does it have to be that tight? It seems like it would be uncomfortable." "Yeah," he answered. "Otherwise, the electrodes don't make good contact with the skin of the neck and the collar flops around when they hunt." I clipped a twelve-foot-long check cord onto Joey's collar, and off we went into the field. Mike steered us toward a clump of oat grass. Joey slowed, stopped, and lowered his head. Catapulted into the air by the DogTra bird launcher, a startled pigeon shot up out of the grass, realized it was airborne, and flapped furiously off toward the bay.

"Did you see him blink that bird?" asked Mike, holding the check cord. "No," I responded. "Did something get in his eye?" "No." Mike was trying hard to be patient. "Blinking is when they sort of shy away from the bird for some reason. He caught the scent downwind, but moved away from it with his ears down. He's had some rough treatment. Probably somebody hammered him." "You mean physically or verbally?" I asked. "Maybe both," he answered. "Could be somebody overused the electronic collar near the bird. Now he associates the bird with a shock. He wasn't havin' any fun."

Mike planted some chukars and said, "Let's try a different kind of bird. He may have a problem with pigeons for some reason." I coaxed Joey toward a clump of oat grass that was upwind of the slight breeze flowing off the bay. He slowed, then froze into a steady point. "Bring him in a little closer," directed Mike. "He could be gun shy. I just can't tell. If you like, I can shoot a chukar over him. It's your call. At least we'll know." I told Mike to go ahead: what was the downside? A chukar popped up out of the grass, cranked up its wings, and accelerated toward the horizon, only to tumble head over heels when Mike's load of

20-gauge shot caught up with him twenty yards out. Joey raced toward the bird, grabbed it, and began to tear around the field shaking it violently. Then he dropped to the ground and worked it over, spitting out feathers from time to time. "Well," observed Mike. "He's not gun shy, that's for sure. See if you can get him to bring the bird on over." I blew a long blast with my whistle, Joey's cue to race over to my left side. Nothing. He continued to worry the bird, plucking more down from its side. "Joey, come!" I commanded. No response. Mike told me to start running back toward the truck while continuing to call him. After a few yards of that tactic, Joey picked up the bird and raced toward me, only to fake past me on the left and end up near a haystack across the road. I yelled, "Joey, come!" three times. The third command brought him back across the road and near enough for me to grab the bird. Later Mike told me he jolted Joey with the collar on the third command—the only time he had used it until then.

After an hour of mixed results, I asked Mike for his opinion about Joey's potential as a bird hunter. "You'll find I'm a pretty direct, honest guy," Mike said. "Good," I answered. "That's what I'm looking for." "I wouldn't spend a lot of money on this dog," he continued, while coiling a check cord. "He's not going to win any national championships. He's a rescue. He may or may not be trainable. What I would do is get him out in the field as much as you can. He just needs to learn that hunting can be fun again. That it doesn't mean a lot of yelling and whacking and jolts from the E-collar. He's got a good nose, that's for sure. Once he learns to discriminate between old scent and live birds, he may do fine." After I told Mike about Joey's habit of squealing when Claire tried to slide him along the sofa, and her snapping encounter with him, Mike said, "That's dominance, pure and simple. He's trying to assert his dominance over her. It's good she didn't let him get away with that."

During a meeting with fellow marine veterans in the spring of 2006, I learned that wounded warriors of the Iraq conflict, including several marines, were being treated for head trauma at the Veterans Administration Hospital in Palo Alto. The staff welcomed visits, I was told, especially from military veterans. It occurred to Claire and me that the natural health-enhancing qualities Brittanys impart to their owners could be shared with these veterans who are in need of special healing. What if we took Joey and Brady down to the veteran's hospital? It might boost the veterans' spirits somewhat and add a unique quality to the visit. After all, recent research suggests that kids raised in households with pets developed more robust immune systems than kids raised in households without pets. Every year produces another report from the Centers for Disease Control proving that dogs lower blood pressure, cholesterol levels, triglyceride levels, and feelings of loneliness. Discounting all the times Joey and Brady had *raised* my anxiety level and blood pressure with outrageous behavior, I was on board with the research and ready to give it a try.

A VA staff member told us we would need certification from our veterinarian that Joey and Brady were free of internal and external parasites, were up to date on their immunizations, and had undergone a personality evaluation assuring they could get along with other dogs and people.

One rainy Sunday afternoon we met the recreational therapist Susan Feighery in the foyer of the Polytrauma Rehabilitation Center in Menlo Park. Right off she struck me as the type of person you'd want to have around if you were working your way back to full functionality, which all of these veterans were. She gave us some background on the VA facility in Menlo Park and the one farther south in Palo Alto. As we neared the ward where we would meet the patients, her optimism and upbeat humor were even beginning to lift my spirits, although there was nothing wrong with me that a new left knee and a restored head of hair wouldn't cure. Spinning their wheels as if they were on pond ice, Joey and Brady pulled us down the polished passageway and into the ward, where we met two marines and a soldier. Marine Gunnery Sergeant Kenneth W. Sargent walked into the room later, accompanied by his wife, Tonya. From her, we learned that her husband was with MSSG 15, a logistical outfit, in August 2004 in a cemetery near Najaf, Iraq. He was riding on an amphibious tractor when a sniper round fired from a nearby building ripped through his right eye socket and shot out the side of his skull. While listening to him talk, I couldn't help thinking that he should not have survived that wound. Yet here he was stringing thoughts together in complete sentences and paragraphs, turning once in a while to have Tonya fill in some blank like the name of the Iraqi town where he was wounded. It is testimony to the stunning efficacy of modern medical science and the rehabilitation practiced in this facility that the following month Sargent reported to active duty with a maintenance unit at Camp Pendleton, the sprawling marine base in Southern California.

While I swapped stories with the gunny and other patients, and signed copies of my Vietnam memoir, *Full Circle: A Marine Rifle Company in Vietnam*, Susan asked Claire to accompany her down the hall with Joey and Brady to see a patient who wasn't responding that well. When Claire looked into the hospital room, she saw an Hispanic man with huge brown eyes lying in bed staring out into space. He looked to be in his mid thirties. Susan said his name was Escobar. Claire brought Joey and Brady closer to the bed, and Susan explained to Sergeant Escobar that the dogs had come to visit him. Escobar's head was turned to the side, and he was staring out the window. Susan said, "This is Joey and this is Brady." Aware that Escobar was susceptible to infection, Claire was careful not to allow the dogs to jump up and scratch him with their nails. Joey being Joey, he rose up, placed his paws on the side of the bed, and peered over at Sergeant Escobar, while Brady made little gerbil noises. "When Brady did that," Claire said, "I picked him up and turned him away, holding him against my shoulder as I approached Sergeant Escobar." That way Escobar could touch Brady's fur without the risk of scratching. At that point the marine turned his head and looked in Claire's direction while trying to move the arm that had been lying immobile next to his body. Claire helped his hand over toward Brady's back and brushed it against his silky fur. Then she told the sergeant that Brady is a bird dog with a lot of energy. He's high-spirited and a lot of fun. He also likes people a lot. The look on Escobar's face convinced Claire that, as she said, "the wheels were turning, but he couldn't communicate." When they left the room, Susan Feighery told Claire through welling tears that she saw a flicker of a smile on Sergeant Escobar's face for the first time since his arrival in the facility. His reaction alone made our trip worthwhile.

At 6:45 a.m. on a Monday morning, with five minutes to go before the commute to San Francisco begins, I'm trying to answer one last e-mail message. With uncanny timing, Joey comes padding in to my office, gazes up at me with those huge amber eyes, and offers his right paw, the idea being for me to massage it before I go out the door. This is the legacy of my once rubbing what I thought was a sore paw one morning some months before. Big mistake. Then he offers his left paw, then his head for a head massage. Given the timing, I suspect it also is his way of saying so long, hasta la vista, until that afternoon when we

hook up for a walk in the hills, rain or shine. The weak light coming through the window illuminates faint frosting on the fur above Joey's eyes; at almost six years old, his eyebrows already are beginning to show signs of aging. Canine massage over, I grab my briefcase and head out the door. On the way to the bus it strikes me that adopting Brady has been a rejuvenating tonic for all four of us. The synergy between Brady and Joey has continued to build, and Brady's effervescent personality has brightened up the place. The little character has taken to biting Joey in the butt when he wants to play, racing around the dining room table at warp speed with Joey right on his heels, down the hallway, into the living room, through the door into the bedroom, then a home-plate slide under the bed out of reach, triggering a flurry of frustrated barking from Joey. From the breakfast table this morning, all I could see through the doorway was a short blur followed by a long blur. After ten minutes of this, they both collapsed on their sofa in the den. I will leave it to Claire to somehow get what she calls the Burrito Brothers off the sofa and down to the backyard before she tools off to her job in Sausalito at 8:30. "Some days it takes one 'Good Boy Cookie' to bribe them," she says. "Sometimes it takes two. On the off days," she jokes, "it would be easier and faster to call AAA for a tow truck."

When Claire and I reminisce about the five Brittanys we've owned, their unique personalities stand out in our minds: Red, the good old boy from Oklahoma, a patient, wise, and dependable companion; Maxwell, the rambunctious outlaw who pushed the envelope until it ripped; Blazer, the spirited adventurer with keen intellect, remarkable sensitivity, and stunning beauty; Joey, the big, lanky Brittany who needs constant validation and reassurance; Brady, diminutive, feisty, and independent, yet intensely affectionate. We both agree that even if we had been destined to have kids in our lives, dogs still would have been part of the picture. Frustrations and expense aside, we would not have had it any other way.

About the Author

William L. Buchanan's articles about dogs, the outdoors, and the military have appeared in *Human Events, Backpacker Magazine,* the *Retired Officer,* the *San Francisco Chronicle,* the *San Jose Mercury News,* the *American Brittany,* and the *Marine Corps Gazette.* His opinion pieces and editorials appear from time to time in the *Marin Independent Journal.* Buchanan is the author of *Full Circle: A Marine Rifle Company in Vietnam.* After serving as an officer in the United States Marine Corps, he joined the Federal Bureau of Investigation in 1969. He retired from the FBI in 1996 and cofounded Cannon Street, Inc., a private investigation firm in the financial district of San Francisco. He and his wife, Claire, live in Mill Valley with two Brittanys, Joey and Brady.